PICKET LINES
AND BARGAINING TABLES

PICKET LINES
AND BARGAINING TABLES
Organized Labor Comes of Age, 1933-1955

By Thomas R. Brooks

GROSSET & DUNLAP

PUBLISHER / NEW YORK

For Chris, Will and Karen

Contents

PICKET LINES
AND BARGAINING TABLES

Introduction

AMERICAN UNIONISM dates back to the end of the eighteenth century. The first workers to organize a real union were the craft-proud shoeworkers of Philadelphia. These journeymen cordwainers, as they were called, banded together in 1794 to protect and defend their special interests as workers. The pride of these individualistic shoe craftsmen was as firmly linked to their work as the leather soles were stitched to the sturdy boots they made. In those days, cordwainers fashioned the complete boot or shoe, whether it was made specially to a customer's order or produced for stock that was sold to the general public. Though the journeyman worked for a Master Cordwainer, who employed anywhere from one to twenty or more men, he often worked by himself at home. Even if he sat at a bench alongside his fellows in the Master's shop, he was free to work at his own pace.

The journeyman cordwainer's independence, however, was being threatened by new ways of shoe manufacture in New England. There, in growing numbers of small shoe factories, the system of piecework had been introduced. Instead of producing the entire commodity, each worker made only a part of it. Some did nothing but cut the leather, while others stitched and sewed the parts separately until the boot or shoe was completed.

These production methods, based on a division of labor among workers, were the direct result of new business opportunities that had developed at the close of the American Revolution. Increased demand for footwear in the South and the West in the post-revolutionary period led to increased competition among shoe producers for these rich and growing markets. The system of piecework sped up production, lowered costs, and made it possible for factory owners to sell their wares at lower prices. Feeling the sharp pinch of competition, the Master Cordwainers also tried to cut costs by pressing their journeymen to work faster and by keeping their wages down.

In 1789 the Master Cordwainers had formed an employers' association to protect themselves from what they termed the "unfair competition" of the shoe factories. It was the journeyman who bore the brunt of this war between the clashing business interests, for the chief method of protection devised by the bosses was to agree on the prices, or wage rates, they would pay their workers. When this resulted in wage cuts, the journeymen "turned out"—or struck—and refused to work until the old rates were restored. To make their strikes more effective, the journeymen, in 1794, created their own protective organization—The Federal Society of Journeymen Cordwainers.

It was the first real trade union in the United States. Workers who refused to join were ostracized and the union men would not work for any employer who hired a non-member. The new union was at first successful, establishing $2.75 as the basic rate for the making of the whole boot. However, by 1804, competition for the new markets became fierce. One employer, for example, reported losses of $4,000 —a good deal of money at the time—in an unsuccessful attempt to establish his business on a sound footing. The Master Cordwainers that year, right after Christmas, cut journeymen wages to $2.50 for the complete boot.

4

The wage cut sparked a major turnout in 1805. The journeymen countered the wage cut with a demand for a raise to three dollars. Strike benefits were paid—fifty cents a week for each person in the journeyman's family. Still, economic want, the necessity of feeding one's family, forced some men to "scab"—to work despite the strike. There were no picket lines as we know them, no marching workers and no "On Strike" signs. Since most of the journeymen did go out on strike and their places of work were widely scattered, picket lines were unnecessary. But strikers in small groups, or committees, did visit the shops of the Master Workmen to see that no one worked. Whenever they found a worker "in," they tried to talk him "out," and if he were unwilling, tempers flared. Though there were no reports of violence, there were some of threatened violence.

The employers retaliated by having George Pullis, a strike leader, and seven others arrested under an old common law ban against conspiracy. The arrests ended the six-week-old strike. Pullis and his fellow workers were indicted for organizing "a combination and conspiracy to raise their wages." The trial took place in March, 1806, before a jury of small businessmen. The jury agreed with the judge, Recorder Moses Levy, who said: "A combination of workmen to raise their wages may be considered in a two-fold point of view: One is the benefit to themselves, the other is to injure those who do not join their society. The Rule of Law condemns both." The eight journeymen cordwainers were fined eight dollars each, plus court costs, and committed to jail until the fines were paid.

The decision came as a shock to the journeymen and wrecked their union by taking away its economic muscle, the right to strike. The doctrine of criminal conspiracy, as set down in the Philadelphia cordwainers case, checked the early growth of trade unionism. It was applied in nineteen cases in Connecticut, Maryland, Massachusetts, New York, and Pennsylvania and was an implied threat that made many other workers cautious about trying to organize. The doctrine was overturned in 1842 in a Massachusetts case (*Commonwealth v. Hunt*) that, as it happened, involved another generation of shoemakers. The court's action allowed for some trade union activity, but the rights of unions under law were not to become firmly established until support of collective bargaining became a matter of public policy in 1937.

Meanwhile, workingmen turned to another form of organization to better their lot—the workingmen's parties of 1828–1830, which spawned some fifty newspapers and organizations in fifteen states from Maine to Georgia and west to Missouri. Unable to organize on the job, workers turned to politics. The new red-brick factories then rising in the industrial regions of the country were an additional reason for worker political action. When Samuel Slater opened the first textile mill in 1790 in Pawtucket, Rhode Island, his work force consisted of seven boys and girls, ages seven to eleven.

Slater's Mill in Pawtucket, Rhode Island was the first textile mill in America.

BROWN BROTHERS

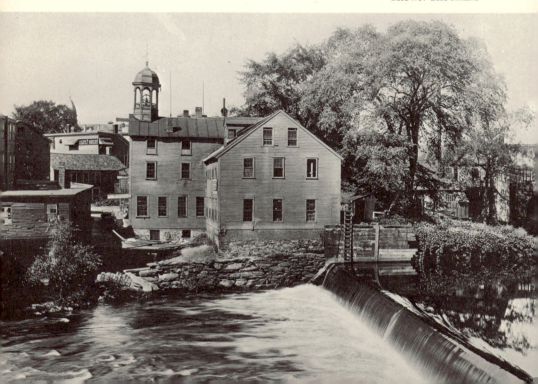

In the mills of Lowell, Massachusetts, girls in their teens worked twelve hours, thirteen minutes a day, or 73½ hours a week. Small wonder, then, that workingmen's parties demanded both an end to child labor and shorter hours of work. This, along with demands for universal free education, abolition of imprisonment for debt, a mechanic's lien law to make wages the employers' first obligation in bankruptcy (a frequent event in pre-giant corporation times), easing of credit, the establishment of a "sound" currency, and land reforms were the issues upon which these parties were founded.

It is difficult today to conceive of an alternative to the factory system. We forget that many once considered the factory system both alien to, and destructive of, American ideals. "The factory system contains in itself the elements of slavery," declared a New England weekly paper, *The Voice of Industry* in 1846. This was a widely shared belief among artisans, workingmen, farmers, and the leading intellectuals of the time, such as Ralph Waldo Emerson, Bronson Alcott, and Theodore Parker. Henry David Thoreau, mulling over the problems of the new age on the lonely shores of Walden Pond, was not the only one to ask, "Where is this division of labor to end?"

It is, as we know from the introduction of the computer into the factory, still going on. Work, therefore, remains central to the American experience. Its changing character has shaped our country from the day Captain John Smith at Jamestown begged England to "send but thirty carpenters, husbandmen, gardeners, fishermen, blacksmiths, masons, and diggers up of trees' roots, well-provided; [rather] than a thousand such as we have now," down to the day in 1963 when AFL-CIO President George Meany cried out before an AFL-CIO convention, "automation is a curse!"

Trade unions were also born of the need of workers to assert some measure of control over their work. Thomas Carlyle, the Scottish historian, once wrote, "All work, even cotton-spinning, is noble; work alone is noble." Yet, work dictated *solely* by the demands of the marketplace, or *only* on terms set by an impersonal corporate employer, or *entirely* paced by the machine robs a man of his dignity and destroys his pride in the quality of his work. Unions, as even a glance at labor history shows, evolved as a response to conditions that threatened the workers' sense of self, pride of craft, and desire for freedom. This is true of the smallest of craft unions, the thirty-one-member International Association of Siderographers (steel engravers), and the largest of industrial unions, the 1.6 million-member United Automobile, Aerospace and Agricultural Implement Workers. And it is just as true of the first union in our history, the Journeymen Cordwainers, down to the latest, the United Farm Workers, which organizes migrant farm laborers in California and along the East Coast from Florida to New York.

The swing from narrow, economic, defensive trade union action (e.g., the cordwainers) to broad-scoped, offensive political action (e.g., the workingmen's parties) works like a pendulum in American labor history, shifting from one phase to the other in a regular, recurring pattern. The influence of government and the courts on trade unionism, for good or ill, also persists throughout our history. It was, as we shall see, decisive in the coming of age of organized labor in the years 1935 to 1955.

The Noble and Holy Order of the Knights of Labor, founded in 1869 by a group of Philadelphia tailors, represented an extreme swing to political action. The Knights dared to dream of a different America, offering an alternative, however tentative, to that set by the plutocracy of wealth, or what Samuel L. Clemens (Mark Twain) and Charles D. Warner called the "Gilded Age," in their novel of the same title. At its peak in 1886, the Knights enrolled a membership of 729,677, the largest ever obtained by organized labor to that date.

The Knights took on the greatest industrial giants in the era of trusts, the railroad barons, and lost. The railroads blacklisted all their workers who belonged to the Knights and thereby broke the union. But the defeat suffered by the Knights was also due to a fatal internal weakness. Its leaders and rank-and-file members were divided between those trade unionists who wanted to build a labor organization strictly rooted in the work place, and those who saw the Order as a

This old print shows police battling with angry strikers in the violent Haymarket riot of 1886.

9

general, all-embracing organization of workers, farmers, and small businessmen that would transform society. The Order's final collapse occurred while it was under the leadership and influence of its militant activists. Significantly, one of the surviving offshoots of the Holy Order was the United Mine Workers.

The principle of craft unionism survived in the American Federation of Labor, which was founded in 1886, partly as a reaction to the loftier aspirations of the Holy Order. The craftsmen wanted to protect what was theirs, not to remake America. The craftsmen were practical and hardnosed about their sources of power. They owned their own tools and worked in local job markets. Their unions, because they were national, proved to be stronger than any single employer within their respective industries. Once organized, for example, the carpenters in St. Louis possessed greater strength than any single Master Carpenter, or for that matter, than the Carpenter's [Employers'] Association in that city. The carpenters, through their union, effectively controlled the job.

Craft pride combined with job control and a benefit system became the basic, underlying strength of the craft unions, enabling them to survive the perilous decades ahead. Just as the sense of solidarity and brotherhood was the revolutionary contribution of the industrial unionists, so control or ownership of the job was the revolutionary contribution of the craft unions of the American Federation of Labor.

The AF of L prospered, reaching a peak membership of 5 million in 1920. Thereafter it came under progressive attack by American industry, which threw all its vast resources of economic power and political influence into the fight against unionism. Armed with court orders barring boycotts, picketing and strikes, and utilizing the so-called "yellow dog" contracts ("I agree I won't join a union on taking this job"), the owners slowly whittled away at the strength and vitality of the craft organization. By 1933 the Federation had declined to a low of 2.9 million members.

The first executive council of the union that was to become the American Federation of Labor. Left to right: (top row) Samuel Gompers, W. H. Foster; (seated) Charles F. Burgman, Richard Powers and Alexander C. Rankin.

The coming of age of organized labor waited on the adoption of a public policy that accepted the picket line as a legitimate way of forcing reluctant employers to the bargaining table where differences over working conditions as well as wages might be resolved. This finally took place in 1935 when Congress adopted the Wagner Labor Act, which guaranteed workers the right to organize, choose representatives, strike, and bargain collectively with their respective employers.

Collective bargaining thus became a recognized instrument

of public policy. As such, it is imaginative, flexible, and an enormously complicated process, ranging from the procedures through which one man may file a grievance against his foreman to the control of investment policies for pension funds that total in the millions of dollars. And, in our age of automation, collective bargaining is sure to become an even more complex instrument of industrial democracy. Collective bargaining gives laboring men and women some say about the conditions of their employment. In 1935, Congress acted to make this desirable condition a matter of national interest. This book, tells the story of what happened in the following two decades, when working men and women sought to take hold of their own destinies.

I. Organize the Unorganized

THERE IS NOTHING LIKE A GOOD FIST FIGHT to attract attention. And John Llewellyn Lewis, the beetle-browed, fifty-five-year-old chief of the United Mine Workers came to the 1935 convention of the American Federation of Labor at Atlantic City looking for a fight. He had started work in the mines as a boy of twelve and knew what a union meant—or should mean—higher wages and better working conditions. He also knew that the Federation wasn't doing the job of organizing the hundreds of thousands of unorganized workers in the mass production industries of auto, steel and rubber. He, therefore, came to the convention an angry man.

Two years earlier, Congress had enacted the National Industrial Recovery Act in an effort to revive the faltering economy. As a result of pressures from organized labor, much of it started by Lewis, two sections were included in the Act: Section 7a, which guaranteed the right to collective bargaining; and Section 7b, which imposed upon the President the responsibility of encouraging "mutual agreements" between employers and employees on "the maximum hours of labor, minimum rates of pay, and other conditions of employment." Such agreements, embodied in National Recovery Administration codes, were more honored in the breach than in the observance. Nonetheless, the ink of Presidential approval had scarcely dried before sound trucks, emblazoned with the slogan, "The President Wants *You* to Unionize," began to roll through the coalfields of Kentucky, West Virginia, Pennsylvania, and Illinois, as well as through the garment centers of New York, Philadelphia, Cleveland, and Chicago. The results were beyond the wildest dreams of even Lewis, who, as *Fortune* put it, "made a noise like the whole labor movement." Within two months, the United Mine Workers added 300,000 members to its ranks, the International Ladies' Garment Workers' Union added 100,000, and the Amalgamated Clothing Workers 50,000.

Elsewhere, workers sought to organize. In Detroit, auto workers rushed into nearby bars after work to quench their thirst and to ask the bartender if they might join his union, any union. Three times as many workers struck in 1933 as in 1932, 812,000 as against 243,000. Increasingly, the issue became the simple one of union recognition. As the AF of L executive council reported in 1934, "Workers held mass meetings and sent word they wanted to be organized."

Lewis became convinced that industrial unionism, that is, organizing *all* the workers within a given industry into *one* union rather than breaking them up craft by craft into many separate unions, was the way to organize the mass of unorganized workers in steel, auto, ship building, rubber, and other basic industries. In particular, Lewis was eager to see the steel industry unionized.

The Mine Workers had just organized the so-called "captive mines," coal mines owned by the major steel companies, and Lewis feared that non-union conditions in the steel industry would be a drag on the progress of the miners. As he later told his biographer, Saul Alinsky, "Every year as we sat down to negotiate with the coal operators, they could . . . justify their unreasonable position [against a wage increase] by citing the lower wages of the unorganized steel workers."

14

Lewis believed that the men in the steel mills could not be organized if they were told "go here, go there," some into the plumbers, others to the sheet metal workers or to the machinists. "We must take them all, or none," reads the field report of a 1930's labor organizer.

At first, Lewis hoped that this might be accomplished within the framework of AF of L "voluntarism," a policy of non-interference with the affairs of the affiliates of the Federation. Once a group of workers obtained a charter it was free to do pretty much as it pleased within its industry, or the jurisdiction of its charter, so far as the Federation and the affiliated unions were concerned. Quarrels over which workers belonged to what unions did take place, but mostly on the fringes of the jurisdictions in question. The International Brotherhood of Electrical Workers, for example, might fight with the International Association of Machinists over workers manufacturing electrical appliances but rarely if ever over workers in a machine shop. Those jurisdictional disputes that did take place were settled on the simple basis of who got there first and/or had the strength to hold on. Lewis and the industrial unionists believed that by securing a charter, say, for the workers in the electrical appliance industry, the electrical and machinist unions would respect the jurisdiction of the new union; and, even if they did not, that the industrial union could hold on to its own.

At the AF of L's 1934 convention in San Francisco, Lewis exacted a concession from the craft-oriented delegates, directing the executive council "to issue charters for national and international unions in the automotive, cement, aluminum, and other mass-production industries. . . ." If the unorganized workers now clamoring at organized labor's half-open door could get charters, then "voluntarism" ought to work in their favor, turning a foothold into rapidly growing mass unions.

But the Federation was in a cautious mood. "What we want," declared Arthur O. Wharton, head of the craft-based

International Association of Machinists, "is to have positive instructions sent out by the American Federation of Labor which will prevent any poaching upon our International Unions." Daniel Tobin, heavy-handed chief of the Teamsters Union, took an even blunter view: "The scramble for admittance is on," he declared in 1934 at the heyday of the NRA. "We do not want to charter the riffraff or good-for-nothings, or those for whom we cannot make wages or conditions, unless we are compelled to do so by other organizations offering to charter them under any conditions. . . . We do not want the men today if they are going to strike tomorrow."

It was an odd position for a trade union leader to take. But the adherents of craft unionism frequently found themselves in similar situations. Consider the experience of John P.

A 1923 meeting of United Mine Workers leaders. Left to right: (back row) E. E. Hunt, C. J. Golden, Pinaldo Cappellini: (seated) Thomas Kennedy, John L. Lewis, John H. Hammond, Thomas R. Marshall, and George R. Smith.

Frey, the president of the AF of L's Metal Trades Department. In 1934, the Mine, Mill and Smelter Workers, an industrial union, struck the copper mines in Butte, Montana. But several of the craft unions, covering only a minority of the copper workers, reached separate agreements with the employers and returned to work, crippling the strike. Frey went to Butte to explain why. His explanation had to do with the sacredness of craft lines. Tall and straight for his sixty-seven years, Frey was visibly distressed when, after he had spoken for an hour and a half, a motion was made to put him out of the meeting hall. According to Frey, the trouble was that the Butte miners hadn't heard a logical argument for years.

Michael F. ("Grandmother") Tighe, leader of the AF of L steel union, kept his union at a manageable membership of 5,000. It wasn't easy, for some 100,000 steelworkers applied for membership during 1933 and 1934. Within the automobile industry, inept AF of L leadership reduced union membership from about 100,000 in 1934, to 10,000 by the winter of 1935. New unions, Lewis charged, were "dying like grass withering before the autumn sun."

So, John L. Lewis came to Atlantic City in no mood for compromise. As he told the delegates, "I was beguiled into believing that the executive council would honestly interpret and administer this policy—the policy of issuing charters for industrial unions in the mass production industries." With his eyes glinting deep within the caverns created by his bushy brows and heavy jowls, Lewis waxed ironic: "They seduced me with fair words. Now, of course, having learned that I was seduced, I am enraged and I am ready to rend my seducers limb from limb. . . ."

The occasion for these Lewisian ferocities was the convention debate over a minority report from the resolutions committee that declared: "In those industries where the work performed by a majority of the workers is of such nature that it might fall within the jurisdictional claim of more than one craft union, or not-established craft union, it is declared that industrial organization is the only form that will be acceptable to the workers or adequately meet their needs." Sturdy Dan Tobin thundered against the industrial union heresy, "and Gompers, McGuire, Duncan, Foster and others said: 'Upon the rocks of trades' autonomy, craft trades, you shall build the church of the labor movement, and the gates of hell nor trade industrial unionism shall not prevail against it.'"

Lewis rose grandly to plead the cause of industrial unionism and to castigate the craft unionists. "Great combinations of capital have assembled great industrial plants . . . in such a manner that they have assembled to themselves tremendous power and influence, and they are almost 100 percent effective in opposing organization of the workers under the policies of the American Federation of Labor." Policies, Lewis declared, that "failed to take into consideration the dreams and requirements of the workers themselves."

"The strength of a strong man is a prideful thing," Lewis warned the delegates, "but the unfortunate thing in life is that strong men do not remain strong. And that is just as true of unions and labor organizations. And whereas today the craft unions may be able to stand upon their own feet and, like mighty oaks before the gale, defy the lightning, the day may come when this changed scheme of things—and things are rapidly changing now—the day may come when these organizations will not be able to withstand the lightning and the gale.

"Prepare yourselves by making a contribution to your less fortunate brethren. Heed this cry from Macedonia* that

---

*The reference to Macedonia is from a passage in the Bible, "And a vision appeared to Paul in the night: there was a man of Macedonia standing, beseeching him, and saying, come over into Macedonia, and help us." Acts 16:9

John L. Lewis talking to a large crowd at a union organizing meeting.

comes from the hearts of men: Organize the unorganized. . . ."

The delegates, however, chose not to heed the cry. The minority, pro-industrial unionism, resolution was defeated by a vote of 18,204 to 10,933.

Though the decision was in, the issue would not die down. It cropped up repeatedly during the rest of the convention.

This 1939 cartoon compares John L. Lewis's new CIO with the latest swing bands while William Green's AF of L is compared to the older style melody band.

20

Lewis took advantage of every opening to make the point that the industrial unionists did not accept the decision of the convention as the end of the matter. As Lewis later pointed out to Alinsky, he sought "an act of some kind, an act dramatic to the degree that it would inspire and enthuse the workers of this country. . . ."

Such an opportunity presented itself on the last day of the convention. A delegate from the Rubber Workers was making a plea for an industrial charter when William L. Hutcheson, the brawny boss Carpenter, reared up, bellowing, "A point of order . . . the industrial union question has been previously settled by this convention." There was a flurry of exchanges. The harassed AF of L President William Green upheld the Carpenters' union chief. Angrily, Lewis rose to thunder: "This thing of raising points of order all the time on minor delegates is rather small potatoes."

Face flushed, Hutcheson jumped to his feet again. "I was raised on small potatoes. That is why I am so small," he shouted with heavy-handed sarcasm.

Lewis walked up the aisle and paused before Hutcheson, whose six-feet three-inches overshadowed even Lewis's formidable 225-pound frame.

"Pretty small stuff," Lewis said.

"We could have made *you* small, could have kept you off the executive council, if we wanted to," the furious Hutcheson replied. He then cursed Lewis, who stiffened and suddenly swung on Hutcheson, hitting him a crack on the cheek bone. The two men grappled ponderously and went down amidst the clatter of collapsing chairs and tables as delegates scrambled to separate the two men.

Hutcheson went off to wash the blood off his face in the washroom. Lewis straightened out his clothes, brushed back his gray-streaked locks and lit a cigar. Casually, he strolled to the platform where a nervous Green said, "You shouldn't have done that, John."

"He called me a foul name."

"Oh, I didn't know that," said Green, ever willing to accommodate. Lewis stared out over the hall.

With one blow, Lewis had dramatized the split within the Federation. A Kansas City union carpenter sent a telegram, "Congratulations. Sock him again." The sentiment was widely echoed. A civil war had been declared. Its outcome would be determined in the mines and mills of industrial America.

II. The House of Labor

THE HUTCHESON-LEWIS FRACAS grabbed headlines. It was so aptly symbolic that it would have made Herodotus, the ancient Greek father of history, happy. There was a lot of history packed in Lewis's punch. Within a year, John L. Lewis would be "Mr. CIO," the leader of hundreds of th usands of workers in the mass production industries rallying behind the upraised banners of industrial unionism. As for William Hutcheson, he was craft-unionism incarnate, or so many believed. Born of Scotch-Irish parents on a farm in Bay County, Michigan, in 1874, Hutcheson was apprenticed to a carpenter in 1901 and joined the United Brotherhood of Carpenters and Joiners of America a year later. He became president of the union in 1915, a post he held until his retirement in 1952 when he stepped down for his son, Maurice Hutcheson.

Hutcheson, however, was no simon-pure craft unionist. Under his presidency, what had been a craft union of skilled carpenters became a craft-industrial union embracing, as a union slogan put it, "All That's Made of Wood Or That Was Ever Made of Wood." By the time of the 1937 AF of L convention, the Carpenters had expanded to include workers in furniture factories and lumbermen of the forests and saw-mills. But discontented, still largely unorganized, lumbermen sought to organize independent of the carpenters. So, it was to protect his own jurisdiction over these and other rebels that Hutcheson rose to block Lewis at Atlantic City.

Still, Hutcheson did personify AF of L conservatism and stodginess in the popular press. Appropriately enough, it was the Carpenters who built the House of Labor, Peter J. McGuire, a carpenter socialist, was the architect and Samuel Gompers, a tough-minded cigar-maker, was the contractor who carried out the job.

Gompers—a short-legged, stocky man with a massive head and face—dominated the Federation for thirty-eight years: from its founding in 1886 until his death in 1924. He was a man with an incredible iron will. Legend has it that he spent his youth reading Marx and other socialist classics to his fellow workers as they rolled cigars. He, clearly, was one of those whom we think of as being born old. Life was not easy for Samuel Gompers. He was born on January 27, 1850, in London of Dutch-Jewish parents. The elder Gompers came to the United States in 1863. At thirteen, Gompers was already an apprenticed cigar-maker.

The young laborer knew poverty at first hand and it inspired his devotion to the cause of trade unionism. "I am a workingman," he once declared, "and in every nerve, in every fiber, in every aspiration, I am on the side which will advance the interests of my fellow workingmen. I represent my side, the side of the toiling wage-earning masses in every act and in every utterance." Gompers soon became convinced that: "The trade unions pure and simple are the organizations of the wage workers to secure their present material and practical improvements and to achieve their final emancipation."

With this single-minded devotion, Gompers guided the Federation through its first rocky decades and on into the twentieth century. Because of this stewardship, most people today credit Gompers with being the founding genius of the

24

AF of L. He certainly epitomized its spirit, which he once summed up before a Congressional hearing. Asked, "What does labor want?" Gompers snapped, "More."

However, it was Peter J. McGuire who undoubtedly supplied the initial philosophy and the tactics that established the AF of L. It was no easy task. Shortly after the founding of the Federation, Thomas Scott, president of the Pennsylvania Railroad expressed the prevailing employer attitude towards labor's efforts at organization: "Give the working men and strikes [sic] gun bullet food for a few days and you will observe how they will take to this sort of bread."

McGuire fashioned an answer to Scott out of craft solidarity. The secretary of the fledgling AF of L was born on New York's Lower East Side in 1852 of Irish immigrant parents. At fifteen, he became an apprenticed joiner and a life-long socialist. The young McGuire fleshed out what little formal education he had by attending free lectures and classes in the evening at Cooper Union.

Executive council of the AF of L in 1920. Left to right: (front row) Daniel J. Tobin, Treasurer; Samuel Gompers, President; Frank Morrison, Secretary; Matthew Wall, Vice-president: (back row) T. A. Rickert, Frank Duffy, James Duncan, Joseph H. Valentine, all Vice-presidents.

After an intense period of activity on behalf of the social-ists, McGuire moved to Saint Louis where he founded the Carpenters' union. Though he held to his belief that the labor movement was "a great democratic training school" for the future management of industry by the workers them-selves, McGuire also came to believe that "every concession obtained is forced by organization *and can be maintained only by organization.*"

The need for an organization that would last brought together the carpenters and cigar makers among other crafts to form the AF of L. "The various trades," states an address by the founders of the Federation, "have been affected by the introduction of machinery, the sub-division of labor, the use of women's and children's labor and the lack of an ap-prentice system, so that the skilled trades were rapidly sink-ing to the level of pauper labor. To protect the skilled labor of America from being reduced to beggary and to sustain the standard of American workmanship and skill, the trades unions of America have been established."

McGuire proposed the drive for an eight-hour day as a way of combining agitation, education and organization. Shorter hours would mean more work, attract workers to the cause of organized labor and create "new wants and aspira-tions and stimulate a desire for better social conditions." May 1, 1886, was the day the millenium was to begin. (This, incidently, is the origin of May Day, an international workers' holiday still celebrated by workers in much of the Free World despite a partially successful takeover by the Com-munists.) Over 340,000 workers responded. For all practical purposes, it was a general strike. What the *New York Herald* said of Milwaukee went for countless cities from Boston to Chicago: "The traditional Sabbath stillness of a Puritan village pervades Milwaukee manufacturing circles. . . . Save for occasional groups of strikers and the rattle of the police patrol wagon on the way to the scene of some disturbance . . . the streets . . . have been deserted."

26

America's first—and so far last—general strike was remarkably peaceful. Initially, it looked like a success. Some 45,000 packing house workers in Chicago, for example, were granted the shorter day without a strike. Some employers, however, resisted. Several hundred policemen wielding clubs broke up a mass picket line outside the Chicago McCormick reaper works. Other workers rushed to join their fellows only to be met by a hail of bullets. Many were wounded; four were killed.

On May 3, a rally was held to condemn police violence. Several of the speakers were anarchists active in the Chicago labor movement. The mayor attended as an observer. He left for home at about 10 p.m., after reporting to the local police station that all was quiet. Then Inspector John Bonfeld, who had a reputation for brutality, marched into Haymarket Square and ordered the crowd to disperse. Suddenly, a bomb exploded among the policemen, wounding 66 (seven died later). Hysterical, the police fired round after round into the stunned crowd, killing several and wounding 200. The identity of the bomb thrower is unknown to this day. The Chicago anarchists were arrested and tried. Although there was no evidence linking these men to the bomb, seven were sentenced to hang; the eighth was sentenced to 15 years in prison. Two petitioned for clemency and their lives were spared; another committed suicide. On November 11, 1887, the rest died bravely on the gallows.

"The bomb," declared Samuel Gompers, "not only killed the policemen, but it killed our eight-hour movement." The Chicago meat packers took away, in the fall of 1886, the eight-hour day they had granted in May.

Still, McGuire had proved his point. Workers would join trade unions, Socialist or not, if the leaders offered the hope of concrete gain. Undaunted, McGuire proposed that one trade—the Carpenters to be the first since they were the strongest—lead the way to an eight-hour day instead of the Federation's once again mounting a general strike. On May

1, 1890, 23,000 carpenters in 36 cities won the eight-hour day, another 32,000 in 234 cities won the nine-hour day. Other building trades unions soon followed suit. These victories assured the success of the newly-formed AF of L. But McGuire's union fell into the hands of fat and sleek, sometimes corrupt, business agents. McGuire drifted into alcoholism and the new men in the union drove him out to die a pauper in 1906.

The Federation, however, was unable to make much headway among the new giants of industry. In 1891, the United Mine Workers sought to carry the banner of the eight-hour day into the coal fields, especially in the coke region around Connellsville, Pennsylvania. But by vigorous use of armed deputies, the mine owners smashed the strike and nearly wrecked the UMW altogether.

The miners' defeat, however, was a mere curtain-raiser for a much more significant clash between workers and the new concentrated power of industry at Homestead, Pennsylvania, during the summer of 1892. On one side were ranged the workers of the Homestead works of Carnegie Steel and their union, the Amalgamated Association of Iron and Steel Workers. On the other side was the chief barony of the new age, the Carnegie Steel Company, a forerunner of United States Steel Corporation, which owned and operated twelve steel and coke works in the vicinity of Pittsburgh, employing 13,000 workers. Henry Clay Frick, the "Coke King," was the new operating head of the company. Under his management, Carnegie Steel, capitalized at $25,000,000 in 1893, would grow to a point where it commanded a price of $300,000,000 from J. Pierpont Morgan seven years later.

At Homestead, located on the left bank of the Monongahela, seven miles east of Pittsburgh, where 12,000 souls lived clustered around the riverside mill, Carnegie Steel turned out with a work force of 3,800, boiler plates, beams, structural steel of all kinds, and armor plate. The monthly payroll totaled $200,000; wages ranged from 14 cents an hour for

28

common labor to $260 a month for skilled workmen. But most of the skilled men made less than $200 a month. In the spring of 1892, the company announced—despite labor negotiations then in progress—a new wage scale pegged to a $23 ton, a figure which represented a wage cut of between 18 and 26 percent. The workmen at Homestead hung Frick in effigy on company property; a hose was turned on the men sent to cut the figure down. Frick used the incident as an excuse to shut down the Homestead works, two days before the old agreement with the union expired on June 30, 1892.

The workers of Homestead picketed the riverside steel mill. They wanted to prevent Frick from re-opening the plant with scab, non-union labor. Their initial moves were

Pinkerton men battle strikers in a violent labor battle at Homestead, Pennsylvania, 1892.

AFL-CIO NEWS

Federal troops were brought into Chicago to quell striking railroad workers during the Pullman strike of 1894.

successful and an alliance with the townspeople enabled them to keep Frick's men out of town altogether. Frick countered by arranging for a boatload of private detectives from the Pinkerton agency to be towed up river on barges. The armed "Pinkertons" were to land and secure the mill. How the workers felt about the strike-breakers may be imagined. Jack London, author of *The Call of the Wild,* once put it this way: "A scab is a two-legged animal with a corkscrew soul, a waterlogged brain, a combination backbone of jelly and glue. Where others have hearts, he carries a tumor of rotten principles."

As the barges neared the shore at dawn on July 5, 1892, the Pinkertons were warned off by strikers. But a plank was shoved ashore and the Pinkertons began disembarking. The steamboat fled downstream, leaving the invaders without means of escape. An unknown person fired a shot providing an excuse for return fire from the armed Pinkertons. Women and children fled out of range. Their menfolk crouched behind the steel scrap stacked in the mill yard and eturned fire. When the Pinkertons finally ran up a white flag that evening, three Pinkertons and seven workers lay dead and scores were wounded on both sides. The Pinkertons were sent back to Pittsburgh, the wounded cared for and the dead buried, and the strikers repaired all damage to the mill.

The strikers won the battle but they lost the war. They held the town but not the industry and certainly not the state government. On July 12, the Governor of Pennsylvania responded to company pressure and sent the militia in to occupy the peaceful town. Other steelworkers went on a sympathy strike. The company retaliated through the courts, securing six indictments—three for murder, two for riot and one for conspiracy. In the fall, twenty-seven Homestead leaders were indicted for treason against the state of Pennsylvania. The men were vindicated by a jury of their peers but their cause was lost. The union treasury was depleted. The Homestead Lodge of the Amalgamated voted to lift the ban against working for Carnegie Steel. Unionism in the steel industry was smashed for twenty-five years.

Appropriately, the last great labor battle of the nineteenth century was a railroad strike that almost became a full-fledged rebellion. By the 1890's, the engineers, the firemen, and the conductors—the highly skilled men—had organized their crafts, on the whole successfully. But the men in the maintenance shops and those who labored on the tracks were without a union. Eugene Victor Debs, then 39 years of age and secretary-treasurer of the Brotherhood of Locomotive Firemen, was asked by some railroad men if he would cast his fortunes with them and help organize an industrial union embracing all lines of work. So, in early 1893, the American Railway Union came into existence. The new union won a brief strike against James J. Hill's Great Northern Railroad. Within a matter of months, the ARU membership grew to 150,000, over one half the combined membership of all the AF of L craft unions.

George M. Pullman, philanthropist and railroad magnate, had constructed, in 1880, a model town adjoining the southern edge of Chicago for his employees who built and repaired his "palace" cars. These cars were leased to the railroads, earning Pullman stockholders and eight percent annual dividend. (The Vanderbilts, who owned the Pennsylvania Railroad, were major stockholders.) During the Panic of 1893, wages were slashed by one-fourth, while dividends were raised by a total of $360,000. (The company also had $25,000,000 in undistributed profits at the time.) The reduced wages ranged from four to 16 cents an hour, hardly sufficient considering that the employees had to pay their paternalistic employer monthly rents of $18 for five room "pens" with conveniences. Rents were cheaper in nearby towns but if you moved, you did not work for Pullman much longer. Chicago supplied Pullman with water at four cents a thousand gallons; the company charged its employees ten cents a thousand. Gas cost Pullman 33 cents a thousand feet but tenants paid $2.25 a thousand. When wages were slashed, prices in Pullman's town were not cut.

Pullman felt that he was a generous man. He might have thought that he was keeping his shops open in 1893 and 1894 as a philanthropic gesture. The wage cuts, he explained, were essential to enable the company to enter lower bids to secure orders during depressed times. Since Pullman had a virtual monopoly—his cars were running on about three-quarters of the country's total railroad mileage—his employees may well have been skeptical about this claim.

However, they accepted Pullman's promises that he would fire no workers elected by their fellows to present their grievances and that the company would investigate shop conditions. But on May 10, 1894, three members of the Pullman grievance committee were fired. By noon the next day, 3,000 Pullman employees laid down their tools in protest. They

A striker in Bayonne, New Jersey fires a pistol shot at a strikebreaker in 1915.

demanded reinstatement of the three men, a return to the old wage scale and reductions in rent. Pullman, the paternalist, was affronted.

The Pullman employees then turned to their fellow workers in the ARU for aid. The union sought some form of mediation or arbitration. Pullman spurned all attempts at conciliation. Against the advice of Debs and the other leaders of the union, the delegates at the ARU convention voted to boycott all Pullman cars unless the company met with a committee elected by its employees. (Debs was afraid that the railroads would use the boycott as an excuse to break the union.) Pullman remained firm. He refused to meet with Debs and other leaders of the ARU and of the strike. The boycott was on. By June 28, 125,000 workers had joined the boycott and twenty railroads were unable to run Pullman cars.

The AF of L, though it backed the Homestead strike, stayed clear of entanglement in the Pullman strike. In part, the Federation did so out of a wish, as Gompers put it, "to maintain the integrity of the Railroad Brotherhoods," which were craft unions, against the industrial unionism of the ARU. But it also kept aloof because it feared the spread of a general strike to sympathetic workers in other industries located in the country's rail centers. Workers in Chicago—and elsewhere—soon passed resolutions to this effect at labor rallies supporting the Pullman boycott. Gompers and other leaders of the Federation, however, feared that such a strike would bring down the House of Labor. It was not an unreasonable fear. Moreover, Gompers was well aware of the fact that it was the tight bonds of craft unionism that enabled craftsmen to survive during decades of murderous class warfare between the new industrialists and their workers. If there were losses, the craft core of trade unionism had to be preserved at almost any cost.

The railroads used their great economic and political power to break the strike, especially by provoking the strikers and their supporters into violence. Scabs were deliberately used to hitch Pullman cars to trains, chiefly to mail trains, that had never before pulled them. There was little violence, however, until President Grover Cleveland, at the instigation of his Attorney-General, Richard P. Olney, a former railroad lawyer, ordered Federal troops into Chicago, the center of the strike, over the protests of Illinois Governor John P. Atgeld. The excuse was striker interference with the U.S. mail. To ensure an angry response, railroad agents infiltrated crowds of striking workers and stirred up trouble. They planted rumors about the movements of Pullman cars and whispered false stories about workers going back to work. When arguments or fist fights broke out, they egged them on. From the back of crowds, they hurled stones at the soldiers. Riots ensued and on July 7, Federal troops fired upon milling, angry strikers and their supporters, killing some 30 persons.

The strike was finally broken by the use of an injunction, ironically issued under the Sherman Anti-Trust Act, which had been enacted in 1890 to curb the excesses of semi-monopolists like Pullman and the railroad corporations. Debs and the ARU leaders were jailed for violating the injunction which barred interference with Pullman rolling stock. The strike was strangled and the ARU totally destroyed. ARU activists lost their jobs and some were barred from railroad employment for a lifetime.

So, hampered by the injunction, American labor entered the twentieth century. Not until the Norris-LaGuardia Act of 1932 were the unions freed of this ominous threat to their very existence.

The years preceding World War I saw the rise in America of reforms stimulated by the seething discontent of the laboring masses in the great cities. Many writers were leaders of reform movements. The social evils festering in the slums were mercilessly exposed by Jacob Riis. In the *Shame of the Cities*, published in 1904, Lincoln Steffens unveiled the greed and corruption that created vast slums. Ida M. Tarbell and Upton Sinclair denounced the trusts, which exploited workers and consumers alike. Because they uncovered so many deeply rooted evils, these crusading writers and journalists were dubbed "muckrakers."

The agitation of the muckrakers, reformers, socialists, and trade unionists soon bore fruit. In 1906, Congress enacted the Hepburn Act to curb the power of the railroads and the Pure Food and Drug Act to protect the health of the consumer. The 16th and 17th Amendments to the Constitution were adopted in 1913, providing respectively for the income tax and the direct popular election of Senators, who were previously chosen by the state legislatures.

By 1912, a considerable body of social legislation governing wages and hours, the employment of children and women, and factory health and safety conditions had been enacted by various state legislatures. The Clayton Anti-Trust Act, enacted in 1914, declared that "the labor of a human being is not a commodity or article of commerce." The Act was an attempt to set aside court decisions applying the Sherman Anti-Trust Act to labor. It forbade the use of injunctions in labor disputes unless a court decided that one was necessary to prevent irreparable harm to property. But the courts quickly seized upon some loopholes in the law and wiped out the gains that had been so enthusiastically hailed by the labor chieftans. Unions were thus forced back into the same weak legal position they had occupied before the passage of the Clayton legislation, when their actions were continually being hampered and frustrated by the law. The stiff price that labor had to pay for this kind of weakness is strikingly illustrated by the case of the Danbury Hatters.

Mill owners in Lawrence, Massachussetts ordered fire hoses turned on strikers during icy weather.

In March, 1902, the United Hatters of North America called a strike and proclaimed a boycott against Dietrich Loewe and Company and its products. The boycott succeeded, and in 1903 the company sued the 240 members of the Hatters in Danbury, Connecticut, for treble damages of $240,000 under the Sherman Anti-Trust Act. Workers homes were attached, pending the outcome of the suit. After fourteen years of legal wrangling, the United States Supreme Court upheld the validity of the suit, confirming a $252,130.90 judgment against the Danbury Hatters. The AF of L spent $98,756.02 fighting the case; the 1915 AF of L convention called for a donation of one hour's pay from union members to aid the hard-pressed hat workers. Altogether, the case cost the far-from-affluent labor movement more than $420,-000. The actual cost, however, was far greater. The fear of suits prevented many workers from forming unions and the AF of L was forced to drop the boycott, a potent weapon in labor's arsenal against anti-union employers.

Just before World War I broke out in Europe, America experienced a general drift towards radicalism. In 1912, the Socialist Party of Eugene Victor Debs racked up its greatest percentage of the total vote cast. And at the same time it seemed likely that the radical rival to the AF of L, the Industrial Workers of the World, founded in 1905, would repeat the sudden growth experienced by the Knights of Labor in 1886 (and in the future that of the CIO in 1937). The IWW was the One Big Union. As William "Big Bill" Haywood, the Bunyonesque IWW leader put it to the founding Convention, "The aims and objects of this organization shall be to put the working class in possession of the economic power, the means of life, in control of the machinery of production and distribution, without regard to capitalist masters."

Their enemies called them the "I Won't Work"; they called themselves "Wobblies," supposedly because some Chinese members pronounced the letter "W" as Wobble. Or,

*Two important early labor leaders, Socialist Eugene V. Debs (left)
and Big Bill Hayward of the IWW.*

it may have been because the letters WW are composed of
several wobbly I's. In any case, as Mortimer Dowling, an old
Wobbly, once put it, it was "the laughing term among us."
And the Wobblies did laugh and sing all over this land.

Itinerant Wobbly soapboxers carried on free speech fights
in San Diego, Spokane, Fresno, Sioux City, and elsewhere.
They organized immigrant silk and textile workers in the
East, harvest hands in the grain belt, lumber and mine
workers in the West, and shoreside and seagoing maritime
workers on both coasts. The kind of job control the Wobblies
won, for example, in Goldfield, Nevada, was the envy of the
conservative craft unionists. The IWW in Goldfield organized every job in town—mine workers, carpenters, cooks
and waiters, and the like. "Under the IWW sway," IWW
secretary-treasurer Vincent St. John later recalled with
pride, "the minimum wage for all kinds of labor was $4.50
a day and the eight-hour day was universal. No committees
were ever sent to any employer. The unions adopted wage

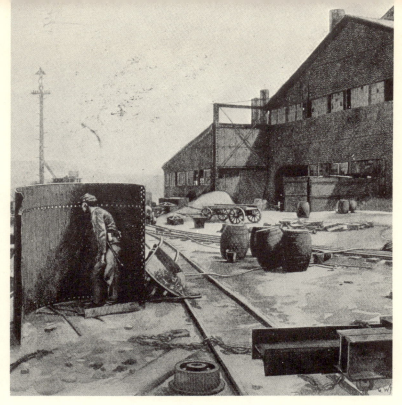

Homestead Strike, 1892. A striker observes Pinkerton men from behind a steel shield. The wheelbarrow is full of nuts and bolts, which workers fired from a cannon.

scales and regulated hours. The secretary posted the same on a bulletin board outside the union hall, and it was the LAW. The employers were forced to come and see the union committee."

But the IWW membership never topped 250,000. World War I intervened, creating a patriotic hysteria that was the undoing of the anti-war IWW. In June, 1917, the Federal government indicted the whole top leadership of the IWW under wartime espionage laws. Over 150 were jailed in that case alone. Altogether, a thousand Wobblies were jailed during this period. Continued harassment destroyed the IWW. Nonetheless, IWW successes in the Lawrence textile strike of 1912 and the Patterson silk strike of 1914, among

39

Union Square in New York City is the scene of this IWW meeting.

others, demonstrated that unskilled and semi-skilled workers speaking many tongues could be welded together to form a fighting organization. It was a lesson that the CIO and John L. Lewis were to take to heart.

Meanwhile, the International Ladies' Garment Workers' Union and the Amalgamated Clothing Workers pioneered a new kind of unionism that had social as well as economic goals. The two needle trades unions were organized by socialists, fervently committed to working class solidarity. This fervor they combined with an imaginative

40

pragmatic concern for the possibilities in a collective bargaining agreement. Their local unions were frequently organized on craft or language-speaking lines (many of their members were recent Jewish or Italian immigrants who spoke little or no English). Through industry-wide negotiations, the ILGWU and the Amalgamated won an entirely new spectrum of gains in employer-financed, union-controlled pensions, health-and-welfare benefits, and the like, that are a permanent part of the fabric of today's unionism.

Although the AF of L reached a membership of two million by 1914, rising from 550,000 in 1900, its existence was still precarious. It was the war and government encouragement of collective bargaining that finally put the AF of L on a more or less permanent footing. Woodrow Wilson became the first President to address a labor convention and to put forward a government policy that stated, in effect, that the right to organize was in the public interest. "We must," President Wilson told the AF of L convention delegates in 1917, "do what we have declared our purpose to do, see that the conditions of labor are not rendered more onerous by the war, but also that we shall see to it that the instrumentalities by which the conditions of labor are improved are not blocked or checked." Wilson had already established a federal Mediation and Conciliation Service, appointed a former secretary-treasurer of the United Mine Workers, William B. Wilson, Secretary of Labor, and was to make union recognition a cornerstone of federal labor policy in war-essential industries where unions already had some sort of beachhead. As these war industries grew, so did the unions. The Railway Clerks bounded from 7,000 members in 1917 to 71,000 in 1919; the electrical workers jumped from 42,000 to 131,000. The AF of L doubled its membership over the same period to 4 million by 1920. The AF of L clearly had reached a point that gave weight to President Wilson's observation some years earlier that no future President would be able to ignore the labor movement.

III. Yellow Dogs, Finks and Nobles

PREOCCUPIED AS HE WAS WITH THE problems of peace after World War I, President Wilson still took time out in May, 1919, to cable from Paris his call for social reconstruction in America. The question of capital and labor, he informed Congress, "stands at the front of all others in every country." To resolve the question, Wilson declared, the country must develop "a new organization of industry," featuring "a genuine democratization of industry" defined as a "cooperation and partnership based upon a real community of interest and participation in control." Workers were to share "in some organic way in every decision" that affected their welfare.

True, the hard words—union recognition, collective bargaining and the right to strike—were missing. The President's formulations were vague where they ought to have been precise. Still, in the euphoria that followed the end of World War I, the unions believed the message to be one of hope. The economic slump that hit the country after the war lasted only three months. The expansion of the automobile industry sparked growth throughout the economy—steel, machine tools, petroleum, rubber, roads, and public construction. The first few strikes of the post-war period ended in victory for the unions. Sixty thousand clothing workers won the 44-hour week; union members in the building, printing and metal trades scored similar successes. The unions continued to grow in membership. In 1918, the AF of L brought together 24 unions with members and jurisdictions in the steel industry to form an organizing committee. A year later, the steel organizing committee reported to the AF of L convention the unionization of 100,000 steel workers. The times appeared ripe for trade union expansion.

There were other omens, however. Out in Centralia, Washington, vigilantes, including some of the "best" people in town, lynched ex-soldier Wesley Everest, a lumberjack who believed that he and his fellow workers had the right to defend their union hall from armed invaders. Still another sign of the times was the sharp rise in the number of strikes and lockouts affecting 1.2 million workers in 1918 and 4.1 million in 1919.

As workers fought wage cuts on the picket line, employers resorted to violence. During the summer of 1919, for example, miners struck to protest a wage cut imposed by the Allegheney Coal and Coke Company at West Natrona, Pennsylvania. One day shortly after the strike began, a group of "deputy peace officers" led by a mine company official rushed the picket line. One striker was mortally wounded. Mrs. Fannie Sellins, a 49-year-old grandmother, and a United Mine Workers organizer, moved some children who were playing nearby out of danger. She ran back to plead with the "peace officers" to stop beating an unconscious picket. They continued, and an officer turned on Mrs. Sellins, knocking her to the ground with his club. She tried to get up and get away. Shouts to kill her came from someone in the crowd. Three shots were fired and Fannie Sellins lay still; a deputy came up and put a bullet through her head. Another deputy picked up her hat, placed it on his head and pranced before the horrified crowd, "I'm Fannie Sellins now." Despite wit-

The F. Scott Fitzgerald family in 1925. Fitzgerald's novels and short stories portray the high life of the 1920's.

nesses, the known murderers were never brought to justice.

We think of the 1920's as a happy time, the Golden Twenties. It was the era of the Flapper (grandmother of the hippies, or a young lady whose behavior and costume was characterized by daring freedom and boldness), the pleasure-seekers of F. Scott Fitzgerald's novels, and a giddy, glittering prosperity. The Stotesburys, a Philadelphia banking family, equipped their bathrooms with gold fixtures—"You don't have to polish them, you know." Calvin Coolidge laconically preached "thrift and industry" from the White House. And the *Wall Street Journal* summed up the time, "Never before, here or anywhere else, has a government been so completely fused with business." Profits rocketed upwards, rising over 80 percent during the decade. The profits of financial institutions rose even higher, at 150 percent. Output per man-hour in manufacturing rose almost 32 percent between 1923 and

44

Representatives of Steel and Metal Workers Union of the AF of L. Left to right: (bottom row) F. E. Langdon, John Fitzpatrick, Harry J. Stahl, William Hannon, James G. Sause, William J. Bowen: (back row) W. M. Walsh, B. J. O'Brien, J. Manley, M. F. (Grandmother) Tighe, J. B. Etchison, W. Chase, and William Z. Foster.

1929. Hourly wages, however, rose only by slightly over eight percent. Indeed, the prosperity of the Twenties was accompanied by heavy unemployment—13 percent of the labor force in 1924 and 1925, 11 percent in 1926, 12 percent in 1927, 13 percent in 1928, and 10 percent in 1929. When out-of-town firms attempted to place advertisements for machinists in 1924, employers in one manufacturing city persuaded local newspapers not to carry them in order to preserve the town's pool of skilled workmen. Those out of work, however, did not have unemployment insurance, or any form of payments, to see them through until jobs opened up again. These were lean years for American workers and for the unions it was a decade of defeat.

45

The steel strike that began on September 22, 1919, signalled the end of labor's wartime fortunes, revealed the weakness of the protection afforded the unions by the Wilson Administration and encouraged employers to push the "open shop," in theory a place where any worker could get a job but in reality a place where union members could not get work.

The AF of L began its drive to organize the nation's steel workers in 1918. Union strategists hoped that the government's wartime endorsement of collective bargaining would be extended to steel. They also believed that the industry would be unable and unwilling to put up with a strike in order to break the union because immediate profits were too important and readily available. (U.S. Steel profits in 1917 alone were over $253 million.)

Labor's chief tactician in the steel drive was William Z. Foster, ex-Wobbly, streetcar motorman and later chairman of the U.S. Communist Party. Foster's plans called for "a hurricane drive" in all the steel centers that would catch the workers' imagination and "sweep them into the unions *en masse* despite all opposition," putting the employers into such a position that "they would have to grant the just demands of their men." Unfortunately, the unions could not move as fast as Foster deemed necessary for immediate success. A conference was called on August 1, 1918, and a National Committee for Organizing Iron and Steel Workers was formed, composed of the representatives of 24 participating unions. John Fitzpatrick, president of the Chicago Federation of Labor and a prime mover in the drive to organize steel, was elected chairman and Foster, secretary-treasurer. Fitzpatrick and Foster hoped to secure through the committee the results of industrial unionism without sacrificing the craft unionism of the AF of L.

The committee's first gains in Gary, South Chicago, Hammond, and Joliet prompted the industry to extend the basic eight-hour day and other minor concessions to their employees. Union organizers moved into Youngstown, Cleveland, Buffalo, Sharon, Johnstown, and Wheeling. The idea was to encircle the steel capital, Pittsburgh, with union strongholds.

The initial response of the steel workers was favorable. They were working a 12-hour day, a 72-hour week, while miners in nearby unionized coal mines labored eight hours a day and 44 hours a week. The industry boasted of high wages—$28.16 a day for steel rollers and $11.92 for roughers —but such wages were enjoyed only by the most highly skilled, less than one percent of all the employees. A Commission of Inquiry set up by the Interchurch World Movement found annual wages of $2,024 earned by 72 percent of the steel work forces in 1919 were inadequate to sustain even a minimum of comfort. According to the Commission, the unskilled, who made up 38 percent of the industrys' labor force, were unable to earn enough to meet a budget for minimum subsistence of $1,456 a year in 1919.

The industry also boasted of an extensive benefits program, which, however, was designed to hold the loyalty of the skilled, English-speaking minority of workers to the companies. But even that was suspect. Stock subscriptions were conditional upon "loyal service"; pensions could be severed by the company for "misconduct"; and employees were turned out of company-owned homes if they dared to strike.

Judge Elbert H. Gary, chairman of U.S. Steel, outlined the steel companies' position: "Our corporation and subsidiaries, although they do not combat labor unions as such, decline to discuss business with them." The nation's largest corporation, he added, stands "for the 'open shop,' which permits one to engage in any line of employment whether one does or does not belong to a labor union." Gary denied blacklisting or firing union men. But President E. J. Buffington of the Illinois Steel Company was franker, "We don't discharge a man for belonging to a union, but of course we discharge men for agitating in the mills."

Text visible in image:
PRACTICALLY SHUT DOWN
ALSO IN LINE
SOLID
McKEESPORT IS almost UNANIMOUS IN Support of NATIONAL COMMITTEE
YOUNGSTOWN O. ALMOST 100 %
NATION[AL]
IRON & STEEL WORKERS
of the American Federation of Labor.
NATIONAL COMMITTEE FOR ORGANIZING IRON & STEEL WORKERS
Samuel Gompers, Chairman Wm Z Foster Secy & Treas.
LOCAL HEADQUARTERS.

A union organizing office posts the latest progress bulletins on its front window.

The investigators for the Interchurch Commission, for example, found that the men elected as local union officers at a Monessen steel plant were marked for firing and reported that in Johnstown "literally thousands of men were summarily discharged." Steel workers responded by demanding a strike. A month-long poll of the 100,000 organized workers showed a 98 percent vote for a strike. Finally, after the companies rebuffed time and time again all efforts for a meeting with union representatives, some 275,000 steel workers quit work on September 22, 1919. Within a week, some 300,000 to 350,000 men were out. Foster estimated that the strike was 90 percent effective.

The companies immediately launched a counter-offensive, decrying the strike as un-American. Race hatred was deliberately fomented in order to break down the solidarity of the many different ethnic groups at work in the industry. Negro strikebreakers were imported from the South. Sherman Service, Inc., a private detective agency hired by the companies, instructed its South Chicago operatives, "We want you to stir

48

up as much bad feeling as you possibly can between the Serbians and the Italians. Spread data among the Serbians that the Italians are going back to work. Call up every question you can in reference to racial hatred between these two nationalities. . . ."

Company propagandists tirelessly promoted the idea that the strike was a rebellion against the United States government. The "U.S." in the title of the chief steel corporation, it was whispered, meant that the company was an arm of the federal government. Giant posters appeared with a giant Uncle Sam pointing his finger at the onlooker from over smoking steel chimneys, urging, "Go Back to Work," "Ritornate al lavoro," "Wracajcie do pracy." The phrase was repeated in seven different languages.

In the end terror broke the strike. Meetings were banned. At Braddock, Pennsylvania, armed deputies ambushed a funeral procession in a working class neighborhood, clubbing the mourners into flight. Although some strikers may have been among the mourners, the funeral had nothing to do

Police search strikers for guns in 1919 Pittsburgh steel strike.

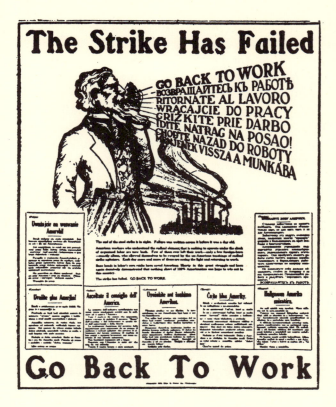

Steel companies ran this ad in Pittsburgh newspapers during 1919 steel strike. Note that the man saying, "Go Back to Work" in eight languages is Uncle Sam, an unofficial but popular symbol of the United States government.

with the strike. At McKeesport, where 3,000 citizens were sworn in as special police deputies, not more than six strikers were permitted to congregate at one time, indoors or out-doors. Mounted policemen rode down strikers' children on the way home from school and clubbed the parishioners of a Catholic priest known to be sympathetic to the strike. Police-men barred strikers from grocery stores in an effort to starve them into submission. Judges handed out jail sentences, offer-

50

ing to suspend them if the victim would return to work. One day in Farrell, Pennsylvania, armed deputies killed three people, wounding eleven others. One woman was shot in the back while on her way to the butcher shop.

An attempt was made to mediate the strike by a group of leading churchmen. It failed and the strike ultimately collapsed. It was called off on January 8, 1920. The steel workers suffered twenty deaths, wage losses between $87,000,000 and $112,000,000 in three-and-one-half months of struggle over nine states.

"The United States Steel Corporation," the Interchurch Commission of Inquiry declared, "was too big to be beaten by 300,000 workmen. It had too large a cash surplus, too many allies among other businesses, too much support from government officials, local and national, too strong influence with social institutions such as the press and the pulpit, it spread over too much of the earth—still retaining absolutely centralized control—to be defeated by widely scattered workers of many minds, many fears, varying states of pocketbook and under a comparatively improvised leadership. The 'independent' steel companies gave the Corporation solid speechless support; not a spokesman was heard but Mr. Gary."

The steel industry's success at maintaining the open shop encouraged employers elsewhere. The missionary work was carried on by a rising number of employer associations. In January, 1921, twenty-two state organizations met in Chicago to promote the so-called American Plan, which was mainly a plan for blacklisting, industrial espionage, and strikebreaking. On December 10, 1917, the United States Supreme Court, in *Hitchman Coal Company v. Mitchell*, held that an individual contract *not* to join a union—the so-called "yellow dog" contract—was valid, that inducement to join a union was a breach of contract, and that strikes where such contracts existed were automatically illegal. Workers who signed a "yellow dog" contract were fired upon joining a union. The court's sanction of the "yellow dog" contract was held in abeyance during the war. But once the country returned to "normalcy" (the end of World War I prompted the Republicans to run Warren G. Harding for the Presidency under the slogan, "Back to Normalcy"), the legalized yellow-dog contract became the employers' chief weapon against the unions and the guts of the American Plan.

The Plan worked. For example, employers in the metal trades utilized the union-busting services of the National Metal Trades Association with such an effect that the membership of the International Association of Machinists fell from 330,800 in 1920 to 77,900 in 1924. The Meat-cutters were all but wiped out in 1921. Total union membership in the United States, at a 5 million peak in 1920, fell to 3.6 million in 1923 and down to 2.9 million in 1933. In 1920, union membership constituted 19.4 percent of nonagricultural employees; by 1930, the percentage was a scant 10.2. The backbone of prosperity in the 1920's, the auto industry, remained non-union and only a trace of craft organization existed in the electrical equipment, rubber, cement, textile, chemical, and food industries.

There were two exceptions to this otherwise gloomy picture—the railroads and the building trades. The former demonstrated the value of government protection of collective bargaining rights and the latter the strength of craft organization in an industry where the worker owned his own tools. In the building trades, the unions flourished through their control over the supply of labor in highly localized markets. The building trades unions actually grew in membership throughout the 1920's, rising from 789,500 in 1923 to 919,000 in 1929. In a second great craft stronghold, the printing trades, union membership also rose over the same period from 150,900 to 162,500.

The fate of the Railroad Brotherhoods was a little different. They actually suffered a decline in membership. But it was

John L. Lewis, William Green and Frank Morrison in front of the White House.

a modest one, from 596,600 in 1923 to 564,600 in 1929. The rail unions were firmly established in the industry when the federal government took over the railroads during World War I. When the roads were returned to private industry in 1920, Congress provided for the continuation of collective bargaining. The Railway Labor Act of 1926 further strengthened the industry's system of labor relations and with amendments the Act has served tolerably well down to the present.

It was a bleak decade for organized labor. Sam Gompers died on December 13, 1924, and William Green became president of the Federation. The choice was an historical accident. When Gompers died, Matthew Woll, a confirmed craft unionist and president of the Photo Engravers, was the heir-presumptive. He made his bid but was opposed by the other strong men on the Federation's executive council, who either wanted the top spot for themselves or, failing that, wanted a man who could be handled by them. No one wanted another Gompers. Green was the compromise candidate promoted for the post by John L. Lewis.

William Green was born on March 3, 1872, of an English coal miner and his Welsh bride, in Coshocton, Ohio. The Green family was large, deeply religious and very poor. William aspired to the Baptist ministry but there was no money to pay for his education, so at sixteen he followed his father into the mines. Later, Green liked to recall that he taught the largest Baptist bible class in Coshocton. He married at twenty-one and became the devoted father of six children. Articulate and dedicated, he soon won office in his local union and gradually advanced within the hierarchy of the United Mine Workers, rising from local secretary to president of the strategic Ohio district of the union, and, later, becoming statistician for the UMW. He became secretary-treasurer in 1913. He served in the Ohio Senate for two terms as a Democrat and sponsored the basic workmen's compensation act of the state. He became an AF of L vice-president in 1913.

The many years spent deep in the mines left marks on his complexion—blue spots deep beneath the skin—and on his character. Green was a decent and humane man with a warm sympathy for the oppressed. For all his devotion to the cause of organized labor, however, Green had the air of a small-town businessman, with his conservative, well-tailored clothes and his gold watch chain lying across an ample midsection. He accepted the craft legacy of Gompers without question, reserving only a mild faith in the industrial unionism of his fellow mine workers.

Green never dominated the Federation the way Gompers so clearly did. However, he was representative of its virtues and some of its weaknesses. During his period in office, power within the Federation shifted from the presidency to the executive council and, in particular, to its more powerful members, including John L. Lewis and William L. Hutcheson. It was the function of the Federation's officers, said Green, "to find a basis of accommodation, harmonize conflicting opinions, to settle differences which arise, not among enemies, if you please, but among the family . . . of organized labor." Green became the great compromiser, the keeper of peace within the House of Labor.

IV. The Blue Eagle

SHORTLY AFTER NOON on October 24, 1929, Charles E. Mitchell, president of the National City Bank of New York, thrust his way through the nervous crowd gathered outside the Stock Exchange and on into the Morgan Bank. He was soon followed by Albert H. Wiggin of the Chase National Bank, William C. Potter of Guaranty Trust, Seward Prosser of Bankers Trust and George F. Baker, Jr., of the First National.

The country's most powerful bankers met for an hour with Thomas W. Lamont, head of J. P. Morgan and Company. Each came prepared to contribute $40,000,000 on behalf of his bank to bolster a tumbling stock market. On his way to announce the pledge to the governors of the Exchange, Lamont met briefly with newspaper reporters. "It seems there has been some disturbed selling in the market," he remarked.

The idea was that the pooled money would be used to buy stocks offered by panicky sellers. This, it was hoped, would shore up stock prices, slow down the selling, and prevent a financial collapse.

The action of the bankers steadied the market, briefly.

Prices held firm, momentarily. But it was the final illusion of a speculators' boom that had puffed Stock Exchange price averages to their highest of all time. The index of 337 industrial stock issues with their average dollar price expressed in points rose from 191.4 points in January, 1929, to peak at 216.1 in September. The price of American Telephone and Telegraph stock rose to $304; General Electric zoomed to $396, having tripled its price in eighteen months. The feverish buying at any price in the expectation that prices would go still higher caused investors to buy "on margin," that is on a down-payment, buy now, pay later system. So, when the air whooshed out of the balloon, panic-striken shareholders, anxious for cash to pay off their borrowings, began dumping shares on the market, selling them at any price. On October 29, 16.4 million shares were dumped; repeatedly, stocks were offered and found no buyers. White Sewing Machine Company stock, which had hit a high in price of $48 the month before, closed at $11 on the evening before October 29. According to writer Frederick Lewis Allen, a messenger boy had the happy thought of bidding a dollar on a block of shares. In the absence of other bids, he got it. The average prices of 50 leading stocks, as compiled by the *New York Times*, fell nearly 40 points. General Motors lost nearly two billion dollars in stock value. By mid-November, the stocks listed in the New York Exchange had fallen over 40 percent in value, a loss on paper of $26 billion.

The spectacular collapse of the stock market obscured the significance of other, more important economic indicators. Industrial production, employment and wholesale commodity indices, were all down by mid-summer of 1929. The tumble of the stock market, however, did speed up the process of economic disintegration. Unemployment mounted at the rate of 4,000 new cases a week. National income, which had topped $87 billion in 1929, slid down to $41.7 billion in 1932. Gross private domestic investment at $15.8 billion in 1929 was down to $1.3 billion in 1933. The Federal Reserve

Board index of manufacturing production tumbled from 110 in 1929 to 57 in 1932. Wage payments collapsed from $50 billion to $30 billion. Unemployment climbed steadily—4 million in 1930, 11 million in 1932, hitting a peak of nearly 13 million in 1933. Small wonder then that playwright Robert E. Sherwood described the years 1929 to 1933 as a "limbo-like interlude between one era and another."

"Have you ever heard a hungry child cry?" asked Lillian Wald, founder of the famous Henry Street Settlement in New York City. "Have you seen the uncontrollable trembling of parents who have gone half starved for weeks so that the children may have food?" As breadlines lengthened and apple sellers occupied city street corners, the Philadelphia Community Council was moved, in July, 1932, to describe its situation as one of "slow starvation and progressive disintegration of family life." And Philadelphia was no exception. In New York City, whole families wrestled with subsistence on $2.39 a week relief money. Toledo allowed slightly more than two cents a meal for the starving. This came out of fast-dwindling city funds. Elsewhere, men ate dandelions, wild onions, and weeds to stay alive.

Meanwhile, businessmen stood fast against the dole (a slightly derogatory term for relief payments to the unem-

The stock market crash of 1929 caused a severe economic depression in America and the world. As unemployment rose sharply, many people resorted to unusual means of making money. Here people sell apples on city streets.

ployed). Former President Calvin Coolidge allowed that it was better "to let those who have made losses bear them than to try and shift them onto someone else." Henry Ford held fast to his belief that unemployment insurance would only ensure unemployment. If the country ever votes the dole, declared Silas Strawn, head of the U.S. Chamber of Commerce, "we've hit the toboggan as a nation." Newspapers featured pictures of wan and sickly Britons "on the dole," implying that living on relief was somehow responsible for the British depression and was therefore something to be avoided at all costs. Yet, the seventy-year-old head of the Baltimore and Ohio, David Willard, was disturbed enough by conditions to blurt, "I would steal before I would starve."

Anger was slow in coming but when it did it was hard and shattering, like the brick flung through a car window one dark night in Gary, Indiana. "What's the big idea?" the driver called out. "All rich guys ought to be strung up," came the answer. "Who are you?" "We're the fellows that'll do the stringing," was the calm reply.

Organized labor was no more prepared for the depression than any other group of Americans. But it responded sooner than most. Unions quickly demanded the thirty-hour week as a means of creating more jobs and called for immediate relief for the unemployed. "The leaders of our organization have been preaching patience," Edward D. McGrady, then an AF of L representative, testified before a Senate Committee in the spring of 1932. But, he warned, "if something is not done and starvation is going to continue, the doors of revolt in this country are going to be thrown open." He berated the Republican administration for talking of balancing the budget. "There are another two B's besides balancing the budget, and that is to provide bread and butter."

If the Administration, he added, "refused to allow Congress to provide food for these people until they do secure work, as far as I am personally concerned, I would do nothing to close the doors of revolt if it starts. . . . It would not be a

During the depression, ramshackle dwellings called "Hoovervilles" sprang up on dumps and urban wastelands. They were "home" for countless dispossessed, unemployed and migratory families in the early 1930's.

revolt against the Government but against the Administration."

That revolt took place in the fall when Franklin D. Roosevelt was elected President. We tend to forget the mood of the country then—in those few months between the election and the inaugural. Perhaps it was best summed up by a banker who declared: "There'll be a revolution sure. The farmers will rise up. So will labor. The Reds will run the country—or maybe the Fascists. Unless, of course, Roosevelt does something."

It was a cold and gray day in Washington, the day President Roosevelt took the oath of office and told the American people, ". . . the only thing we have to fear is fear itself— nameless, unreasoning, unjustified terror, which paralyzes needed efforts to convert retreat into advance."

Unquestionably, the new President evoked a response. He struck a note of hope and challenge that heartened the whole country. But the myth that claims that it was he alone who spurred the nation to action is not entirely true. Even before he took office, the people had already begun to move, taking their own destiny into their own hands. When banks foreclosed mortgages and put farms up for sale at auction, gaunt farmers, armed with shotguns, kept the bidding down to one dollar, for one man—the dispossessed owner. The unemployed demonstrated, organized and marched. Socialists and radicals

Under Roosevelt's "New Deal," the National Recovery Administration was symbolized by the "Blue Eagle" emblem.

of all persuasions organized unemployed councils. In Seattle, shoemakers, carpenters, tailors, laborers worked at their trades in return for wood, fish, apples, and potatoes. By the end of 1932, there were well over 100 self-help and barter organizations in nearly 30 states. Many developed their own script for barter.

Still, such efforts did not fill the desperate need for jobs. Federal action was necessary. Bankers and industrialists put their proposals for recovery before the new Congress. These proposals aimed at halting the drastic fall in prices—and profits—by suspension of anti-trust laws and allowing manufacturers to get together, under government supervision, for the stabilization of prices and production. The unions insisted that recovery plans must be national in scope. Even that staunch conservative labor leader Matthew Woll called for "national planning which will conceive of the economic activity of the nation as a whole rather than individual parts." Organized labor was determined that working men and women should not pay the price for recovery in low wages and long hours. Sweatshops were already springing up around the country. In Pennsylvania, half the women in the textile and clothing industry were earning less than $6.58 a week, and 20 percent less than $5.

The result of these pressures from industry and labor was the National Recovery Act enacted on June 15, 1933. The Act sought to foster industrial self-government under a National Recovery Administration and its famous "Blue Eagle" codes, so called after the blue NRA symbol, the American eagle as it was on a twenty-five cent piece. Even before the advent of the New Deal, the Norris-LaGuardia Act of 1932 freed the unions of injunctive restraints leveled by federal courts against boycotts, picketing and strike action. Yellow-dog contracts were no longer enforceable in federal courts. Section 7a of the NRA went a step further to guarantee the right of collective bargaining and Section 7b imposed on the President the responsibility of encouraging "mutual agreements" between employers and employees on the "maximum hours of labor, minimum rates of pay, and other conditions of employment." Such agreements were to become a part of the NRA codes.

Workers were quick to take advantage of opportunities afforded them under the protection of the Blue Eagle. At the Philco Radio plant in Philadelphia, lively twenty-one-year-old, James B. Carey, organized a Walking, Hunting and Fishing Club. Before long the club transformed a company sponsored employees' organization—what workers called with scorn, "company unions"—into a trade union. The new union asked for a contract, insisting that the NRA made collective bargaining national policy. The company refused but agreed that word to that effect from NRA administrator, General Hugh S. Johnson, would change its mind. Carey and a group of his fellow workers immediately set off for Washington in two rattly old cars. On the way, they bought a newspaper and tore out a picture of General Johnson. Once in Washington, they systematically searched the Commerce Building, opening doors and comparing the faces of the startled occupants with that in the newspaper clipping, until they found a square-jawed face that fit the picture. After outlining their case, Carey demanded, "Haven't we got law on our side?" Johnson agreed. "Well, then," said Carey, "sign your name. Management won't take our word for it." The NRA administrator signed. The exuberant unionists returned to Philadelphia where they swept a somewhat startled Philco management into a closed-shop agreement, a 36-hour week and pay increases ranging from 69 to 150 percent over the old rates.

Other would-be unionists were not quite so fortunate in their managements as Carey and his fellows. They had to fight. Three times as many workers struck in 1933 as in 1932, 812,000 as against 243,000. Increasingly, the sole issue became union recognition under NRA codes.

Congress, declared the *United Mine Workers Journal,* "has given labor the greatest opportunity it has ever had to work out its own destiny." But, warned the *Journal,* "The bill will only be helpful to those who help themselves." The union dug deep into its treasury and staked survival on a summer organizing drive. Sound trucks, emblazoned with signs saying, "The President Wants *You* to Unionize," invaded the coal fields of Kentucky, West Virginia, Pennsylvania, and Illinois. Miners sang:

> In nineteen hundred an' thirty-three,
> When Mr. Roosevelt took his seat,
> He said to President John L. Lewis,
> In union we must be.

Within two months, 300,000 miners joined the UMW, bringing the union back to its 1920's strength of 400,000.

Other workers formed unions. Between 60,000 and 70,000 joined unions in the Akron rubber plants and near-by industries. Almost 200 local unions with 100,000 members sprang up in the nation's auto plants. Lumberjacks and sawmill workers of the Northwest organized 130 local unions with 90,000 members. Aluminum, steel and textile workers requested AF of L charters. Within two months, the International Ladies' Garment Workers' Union added 100,000 to its ranks and the Amalgamated Clothing Workers, 50,000.

"There was a virtual uprising of workers for union membership," the AF of L executive council reported to delegates at the 1934 convention. "Workers held mass meetings and sent word they wanted to be organized." AF of L President Green cried out that he had nailed to the Federation's masthead the slogan, "Organize the Unorganized in the Mass Production Industries."

Ominously, however, for organized labor, there were signs that the NRA wasn't all that it appeared to be. In the year-and-a-half from summer 1933 to winter 1934, troops were called out in sixteen states to be used against workers' attempts at organization. Josephus Daniels wrote President Roosevelt from North Carolina, "Mill men put arms in the hands of the men in the mills and the Governor called out the State Guard, at the request of the owners. . . . In nearly every instance the troops might as well have been under the direction of the mill owners."

Workers, however, scored some victories but at a great cost. A general strike, that is, a city-wide strike of all or nearly all workers, provoked federal intervention in the San Francisco dock workers' strike of 1934. A Blue Eagle board awarded the union recognition, raised longshore pay and established a joint labor-management hiring hall. In Toledo, Ohio, tin-hatted National Guardsmen protected strikebreakers at bayonet point at the Electric Auto-Lite Company plant. Showered by beer bottles and bricks, the Guardsmen opened

Striking Minneapolis Teamsters use clubs, metal bars and links of pipe against police who tried to keep strikers from blocking truck movement in the Minneapolis market area.

fire, killing two and wounding hundreds. The threat of a general strike, however, brought the company around. Federal mediators helped work out a settlement acceptable to both parties. The union won recognition. In Minneapolis, the Teamsters Union all but tied up the entire city—at a cost of 67 wounded, two dead—before winning recognition for in-city truck drivers. The Minneapolis Teamsters organized a District Drivers' Council to coordinate the activities of truck driver locals throughout the region and to win the first uniform contract for over-the-road drivers in 1938, a prototype of the present Teamsters' "master" agreement.

Significantly, in each instance where workers won some gain, the Federal government intervened, not so much on the unions' behalf but as a counterweight to the overwhelming power possessed by the employers. But the use of Federal power was more often than not halfhearted and ineffectual. The textile workers experience under NRA was much more typical of what happened than the events in either San Francisco or Minneapolis.

The textile code was the first to be adopted and it was called a "model." It fixed a forty-hour week and wages of $13

Military guardsmen about to take cotton mill strikers to a military interment camp near Atlanta. Guardsmen were called in to allow non-strikers to cross picket lines.

a week in the North and $12 a week in the South. But actual wages, according to a Department of Labor survey, averaged $10.86 a week. Workers complained of a speed-up, "a stretch-out" that increased the work load from 33 to 100 percent. Despite the protections of the Blue Eagle, 4,000 workers were fired by the summer of 1934 for union activity. NRA administrator Johnson sanctioned a 25 percent curtailment in production that brought pay for a full week's work down to $7.09.

In August, 1934, delegates to the United Textile Workers convention voted to call an industry-wide strike for a thirty-hour work week without loss in pay, the establishment of a maximum work load, an end to the stretch-out, and re-instatement of all workers fired for union activity. The response to the union's strike call was electric. By September 3, 364,795 men and women were out on strike. "Flying squadrons" of union volunteers rode from town to town in battered trucks and old cars. Young and old, men and women flocked out of the mills to greet them and join the strike.

Employers struck back with all the violence at their command. In Fall River, Massachusetts, police used tear gas and

Unemployed auto workers flee when police use tear gas bombs to break up demonstration near the Ford Plant in River Rouge.

pistols to scatter pickets; at Trion, Georgia, three strikers were killed and 14 wounded when deputy sheriffs fired on a picket line. Six workers were killed by deputized thugs in the little mill town of Honea Path, South Carolina.

Eleven thousand National Guardmen were arrayed against the strikers in eight states. At High Point, North Carolina, six strikers were bayoneted by the militia. Workers at Saylesville, Rhode Island, were so enraged by the shooting of two pickets that they took on the armed militia with bare hands and stones from the street. Governor Eugene Talmadge of Georgia declared martial law in strike centers and set up concentration camps for pickets charged with disorderly conduct.

Starvation and terror worked upon the strikers. And President Roosevelt cajoled the union into calling off the strike with the promise of a new cotton textile labor board to investigate standards. He also requested the employers to refrain from discrimination against active strikers. At first the union leaders hailed this as a victory. But disillusionment soon set in. Despite the President's request, 15,000 textile trade unionists were refused re-employment as a lesson to all the rest. "We believed," strike leader Francis Gorman stated before the House Labor Committee, "we had a government guarantee of certain things which meant victory to us. [But] decrees issued by governmental agencies since the strike was ended have been so flagrantly disregarded by so many employers that the spectacle is scandalous and astounding. . . ." The union, which began the strike with a membership of over 300,000, reported in late 1934 a membership of 79,000.

Workers began, not without reason, to call the NRA "the National Run Around." Despite its guarantee of collective bargaining, employers were free to break unions almost at will. Barbed wire fences and sandbag fortifications were set up around industrial plants to keep off union organizers. Hoods and thugs sworn in as special deputies swaggered through the streets of company towns. From January, 1934, to July, 1936, General Motors spent $994,855.68 on an industrial spy system to forestall unionization. The Senate Committee on Education and Labor, chaired by Senator Robert M. LaFollett, estimated that American industry spent at least $80,000,000 on labor spies and anti-union agents in 1936 alone.

Employers, too, were successful at securing court interpretations of the NRA that favored company unions, which flourished in the steel, rubber, petroleum, and chemical industries among others. By the spring of 1934, one-fourth of all industrial workers—roughly ten million—were employed in plants with company unions. Almost two-thirds of these were organized under NRA auspices.

Secretary of Labor Frances Perkins toured western Pennsylvania in August, 1933. At Homestead, she spoke to a group of steel workers at a public meeting, or so she thought. Afterwards she learned that other workers, denied entrance to the hall, were waiting to speak to her outside. Turning to the mayor, she asked that they be invited in. "No, no, you've had enough," said the mayor. "These men are not any good. They're undesirable Reds." Madame Perkins then went outside to speak to the waiting men. At her heels, the mayor shouted, "You can't talk here. You are not permitted to make a speech here." Madame Perkins suggested a nearby public park. The red-faced mayor spluttered, "You can't do that." Finally, Madame Perkins spotted an American flag flying over a building across the street. She led the crowd of workers into the post office where she climbed on a chair and asked for questions about the NRA steel code.

One can imagine the treatment afforded a union organizer or the worker brave enough to speak his mind in such towns if such a personage as Madame Perkins had difficulty. Indeed, terror and economic intimidation ruled over much of industrial America. The Blue Eagle failed to live up to its promises. Out of that failure came the dissension that split the American Federation of Labor. And a frustrated John L. Lewis was the force that split it.

V. John L.

JOHN LLEWELLYN LEWIS, whose massive figure dominated the coming of organized labor, was a man of many contradictions. His outlook in fact was closer to that of the man he punched, Big Bill Hutcheson, than it was to the men he gathered around him in the building of the CIO. He was a Republican, suspicious of government intervention into the affairs of men. Yet, he was an architect of a labor policy that made government a third, if sometimes silent, partner to collective bargaining. He split the AF of L to found the CIO, and was exceedingly ambitious, or perhaps, some say, power hungry. Yet, he resigned in a huff when American workers disregarded his advice to vote against Franklin D. Roosevelt in 1940, although he could have held the reins of power with little or no effort. He returned to the American Federation of Labor, briefly, only to withdraw his United Mine Workers union into isolation and relative obscurity. For a time, his was the authentic voice of organized labor; dramatic, often prophetic, and always at center stage. In the end, Lewis simply faded out of history into silent retirement. Historian Arthur M. Schlesinger, Jr., finds him puzzling. Perhaps, though reporter James A. Wechsler thought it a dramatic oversimplification

Lewis was not far wrong when he told Wechsler, "Think of me as a coal miner, and you won't make any mistakes." In her miners' song, "Which Side Are You On?", Mrs. Florence Reece wrote, "My daddy was a miner/And I'm a miner's son." It's something you don't forget—not if you are a coal miner.

Today, when furnaces are fired by oil or gas more often than not, and when the age of atomic energy seems close at hand, it is difficult for us to conceive of the overwhelming importance of coal. Water power opened the way for the industrial revolution but coal fired its progress, building up such a head of steam that it transformed our civilization in less than a century. As the great English economist, Alfred Marshall, noted, coal enabled the poor to keep "themselves warm indoors without living in an unwholesome and stupefying atmosphere"; it provided power for the looms of England that made "cheap underclothing, without which cleanliness is impossible for the masses of the people in a cold climate"; and as cheap fuel for steam-powered transportation and communications, coal rendered "possible the civilization for the masses in countries the climate of which is not so warm as to be enervating . . . [and prepared] the way for true self-government and united action for the whole people, not merely of a town such as Athens, Florence or Bruges, but a broad country, and even in some respects, of the whole civilized world." Coal, perhaps, was not so essential in the United States where there was an ample supply of water power and wood enough for cheap fuel. Yet, it was not until 1900, when coal production here equaled that of Britain, that our country became a serious competitor for world trade. Even today, coal remains an important resource, providing 66.4 percent of all fuel consumed in the production of electricity. In 1966 coal-powered steam produced 54.2 percent of our electricity.

There is another side to the coal story, "the damnation of

"The mine is a darkness dripping with an oily black slime; a tunnel wracked by the ripping of the cutting machine as it eats into the coal, the whir of drills, the blast of explosives and the constant clatter of coal. . . ."

the mines." Emile Zola catches in *Germinal* the despair of defeated strikers driven back to the mines by hunger. "Everywhere, in the morning haze, along the roads lost in darkness, the flock was tramping on, rows of men trotting with faces bent toward the earth, like cattle led to the slaughter-house. . . . And in this wholesale return to work, in the mute shadows, all black, one felt the teeth clenched with rage, the hearts swollen with hatred, a simple resignation to the necessity of the belly."

Mine owners made huge profits from the employment of teen-age boys and men crouched on their knees forever hacking at the coal face. Coal magnates were impervious to the sufferings of their employees. During the coal strike of 1900, George F. Baer, president of the mine-owning Philadelphia & Reading Railroad, derided reports of the miners' misery: "They don't suffer. Why, they can't even speak English!" The advent of machinery eased the miners' burdens somewhat. Still, there remained the ever-present coal dust, sweat-mixed, streaking the body and drawn into the lungs with every breath. The mine is a darkness dripping with an oily black slime; a tunnel wracked by the ripping of the cutting ma-

71

chine as it eats into the coal, the whir of drills, the blast of explosives and the constant clatter of coal. As evoked by the last stanza of Louis Untermeyer's "Caliban in the Coal Mines" there is:

> Nothing but blackness above
> And nothing that moves but the cars . . .
> God, if you wish for our love,
> Fling us a handful of stars!

"The miner," as Saul Alinsky notes in his biography, *John L. Lewis,* "knows that he digs death as well as coal, and the death tonnage is appalling." From 1910 to 1945, 68,842 miners were killed and 2,275,000 injured. There isn't a mining town without its widows and orphans of men murdered by King Coal. Death is all about the miner deep in the bowels of the earth. It is over his head, coming down with the collapse of the roof in sudden crushing burial. It is in the damp, noxious gas snuffing out lives or exploding in incandescent fury. Rescued after a mine accident, Étienne, the hero of *Germinal,* "appeared fleshless, and his hair was quite white." At the sight, "people turned away and shuddered." Outside the pithead, they lined up the corpses "crushed, with brainless skulls and bellies swollen with water."

Yet, there is something about mining that makes a miner's life a proud one. When he was 12 years old, John Brophy, born in England in 1883 of a miner's family, entered

Women and children wait for news of their husbands and fathers trapped by the mine disaster at Cherry Hill, Illinois in 1909.

a Pennsylvania mine as his father's "new buttie" or partner. (Miners worked in pairs in those days and still do in some places. And partners were called butties according to Brophy.) If breaking in at the coal face was hard on the boy, it was not easy for the man. Brophy's father had to make up for his son since both were rated as equals on the job. No allowance in the tonnage per day was made for the youngster learning his job at his father's side.

During the latter half of the "Gay Nineties," the Brophys moved every few months in the search for work. Discouraged at 16, Brophy decided to follow those who were leaving the mines for the factory. Through an uncle, he found work in a glass factory near Pittsburgh. He worked as a "carry-over," six hours on, six off—twelve hours work in every twenty-four.

A machine moulded a tumbler, then dropped it on a tray held by Brophy. "I walked two steps to my left and placed it on a metal table," Brophy recalled many years later in his autobiography, *A Miner's Life*. "Then I went back and did it all over again—and again, and again." At this distance, the job does not seem particularly onerous for a youngster. But for Brophy it was "an existence of weariness and boredom. I was glad to follow my father back to the mines, where we had some variety in our work, and could, within broad limits, set our own pace."

This decision was characteristic of the man who later became John L. Lewis's major adversary within the mine union and director of organization of the CIO. It was also characteristic of miners. The miner's own pace was no easy one but it was his. Significantly, as Brophy shows in a marvelous chapter on the work of the miner, the miner's pace was set by "the discipline of the work of his fellows." It was cooperative yet it allowed for the individual. "Nobody could work in this kind of situation, where every man had to depend on every other man, if he was not respected as a miner."

For the miner, his union is a way of life. Mining towns are isolated, close-knit communities. And, the union hall is at the center in much the same way the white-washed, steepled church was in the New England town. Old timers who can remember the bitter days when the union was smashed, ineffectual in the face of the superior power of the coal barons, call it a time "when a miner was not a man." Their devotion to John L. Lewis turned on his salvaging the union in the depression, when it took, as they say, "something of a man."

John L. Lewis was born on February 12, 1880, of Welsh parentage in Lucas, Iowa, a small mining community. His father, Thomas Lewis, worked all day in the coal mine and spent much of his spare time helping to organize his fellow workers into the Knights of Labor. When the infant John was two, Tom Lewis was blacklisted for his part in a strike. The strike was successful but not enough so to get Tom Lewis his job back. Until the blacklist was lifted in 1897, the growing Lewis family—six sons and two daughters—moved repeatedly throughout the Midwest as the senior Lewis shifted from job to job in the effort to support his family. As a boy of twelve, John L. sold newspapers, took up baseball and quit school before finishing the eighth grade. At fifteen, he was in the mines, helping to support his family.

When he was 17, the Lewis family returned home to Lucas. The blacklisting of the elder Lewis was ended—whether through union efforts or just because of the passage of time remains uncertain. John, his brother, and father all went to work for the Big Hill Coal and Mining Company. Many years later, a neighbor who worked in the same mine, Robert Wilkinson, recalled, "Lewis drove mules—pulled coal for me at the Big Hill. He was a hard worker. He was a good man—and his folks were nice." The mines were not ventilated in those days. "The air was generally pretty thin," added Wilkinson. "We came home more than one day because there wasn't any air in the mines."

Work, however, could not absorb young John's boundless energy. He organized and managed a debating team and a baseball team. He also managed to sponsor traveling shows

74

ranging from Shakespearian road companies to performing dogs. He read avidly and widely, though erratically, until he met Myrta Bell, the daughter of the Yankee doctor in town. She organized his reading habits and introduced him to Homer and Dickens. The Bible and Shakespeare were already staples in the young Lewis's reading diet and were to remain so for the rest of his life.

At twenty-one, John L. picked himself up and left home for five years. "I suppose if we talk about formal education," Lewis told his autobiographer Alinsky, "I would count that five years as my education." Lewis mined copper in Montana, silver in Utah, coal in Colorado, and gold in Arizona. He swam across the turbulent Big Horn River in Wyoming at high flood, an exploit that nearly cost him his life. In Hannah, Wyoming, he helped carry out the torn bodies of 236 coal miners killed in the Union Pacific Mine disaster of 1905. This experience, along with the silicosis that shadowed the later years of his father, inspired Lewis's life-long passion for mine safety legislation.

In 1906, Lewis returned to Lucas, where he married Myrta Bell a year later. Already exceedingly ambitious, Lewis decided that he needed a broader base than Lucas if he were to advance in life. So, in 1909, the Lewises moved to Panama, Illinois, the heart of the Montgomery coal fields. "Lewis from Illinois," wrote Alinsky, "would mean more to the miners than Lewis from Lucas, Iowa."

Lewis's judgment was accurate as well as acute. With the help of his five brothers, who made an impressive "claque", applauding every Lewis move, he soon took over the leadership of the Panama local of the UMW. He was not only president of the local but its one-man grievance committee. Later, he became state legislative representative for the mine union. After a mine explosion that killed 160 miners, Lewis single-handedly bullied the state legislature into passing safety legislation and a workmen's compensation law. This achievement brought him to the attention of Samuel Gompers, who was looking for allies within the mine union. (The socialists and the miners were Gompers' two greatest opponents. Gompers had only been defeated once in his career and that was by UMW president John McBride in 1895, who had socialist backing.) In 1911, Gompers appointed the husky miner a field representative and legislative agent for the AF of L. The burly Welshman and the stubby Dutch-English Jew made a curious pair. Lewis often acted as Gompers' bodyguard, protecting him from harm whenever the old man went on an occasional carouse. Lewis learned much from the crafty AF of L tactician in those early days of their association.

Once while he was still in the mines, Lewis allegedly was attacked by a half-crazed man-killing mule, Spanish Pete. He reportedly felled the mule with a blow of his fist and finished him off with an iron bar. Realizing that the act might cost him his job, Lewis covered the mule's wounds with clay and reported to the mine boss that the mule had died of heart failure. With that same mixture of brute strength and quick thinking, Lewis built a strong personal machine within the UMW· while on the AF of L payroll. He travelled widely through the minefields, was lavish with his expense account, and became friends with key mine leaders throughout the country. He prevailed upon the then UMW president John P. White to appoint him statistician and business manager of the UMW *Journal* in 1916. Both jobs were sinecures, easy jobs enabling Lewis to continue politicking within the union. Subsequently, Lewis was named a vice-president of the union by UMW president Frank Hayes, an ineffectual alcoholic. Lewis ran the union behind the scenes, becoming president in 1920 of the largest single union within the AF of L., with a membership of 500,000.

Gompers, it was said, groomed Lewis to be his successor. But in 1921, flushed with his succession to the UMW presidency, Lewis challenged the old man. In view of the events

76

of the 1930's, it was an ironic try. Lewis was backed by the so-called "Indianapolis group" of unions, chief of which was the Carpenters. To win over the support of the Socialist-led unions, critical of Gompers, Lewis electioneered on a platform that called for the government ownership of the mines (Lewis later scuttled this plank within his own union) and the railroads, for a program of health and unemployment insurance and old-age benefits. It was a radical program for those days. Lewis, however, did not have the solid backing of his own union and was defeated by a vote of two to one. Just about all he succeeded in doing was to blast forever

Samuel Gompers (right), President of the American Federation of Labor and John L. Lewis (center), then President of the United Mine Workers, and later head of the Congress of Industrial Organizations.

John Brophy, drummed out of the UMW by John L. Lewis, later returned to serve as Executive Director of the CIO for almost thirty years.

his chance to succeed Gompers when the old cigar-maker died.

By then, Lewis was in serious trouble within his own union. The war-time coal boom collapsed and brought open warfare to the coalfields between the union and the operators and later among union members themselves. The opposition within the UMW came together for a time around the gentle figure of John Brophy. The contrast between the two men points up the forces that went into the making of Lewis—and the CIO.

Brophy joined the UMW at 15. Because he quickly won respect as a miner, he was soon elected a checkweighman in the first of a series of elections that would take him out of the mines and into a life of service to the labor movement. The elected checkweighman kept a tally of the coal mined and credited to each miner. As the men were paid by the ton, it

78

was a post of trust. The coal miners chipped in to pay for the checkweighman, who was there to keep an eye on their interests and on the weight boss who was employed by the mine owners.

Self-educated like many a miner, Brophy always remained true to his vision of himself as a "habitual rank-and-filer." He was devoted to the cause of the men—"I had lived my life in mining towns and seen how effective the union could be in correcting evils in both mine and community . . . I formed the habit of subjecting all ideals to the test of my practical experience as a worker and a unionist."

Brophy was a life-long Catholic who was attracted to the Socialist Party, which had a strong group in those days before World War I among the mine workers. But the Socialists never quite won him over. When James Maurer, president of the Pennsylvania Federation of Labor and a life-long Socialist, argued for the formation of a labor party or, failing that, sought endorsement of the Socialist Party candidates, Brophy took the position that "much more education was necessary before endorsement of a minority party could be more than an empty gesture. The idea of a labor party based on the masses of the workers appealed to me, but I felt we were far from ready even for that move."

In 1924, Brophy was one of the few labor leaders who, having endorsed Senator Robert M. LaFollette for the presidency, felt that the labor movement ought to have kept on trying to build a party of its own. In this, of course, he was in agreement with the Socialist Party. But other unionists were more easily discouraged, even though LaFollette rolled up an impressive 4.8 million votes.

Long before this, however, Brophy had been elected president of the important central Pennsylvania District 2, UMW. (Nanty Glo, a colorful name for a grim huddle of houses barely a town, along Black Lick Creek, overshadowed by slag piles, became Brophy's home local.) It was a key district within the union and Brophy soon became a major figure.

Leaders of the anthracite miners meet in the mid 1920's to decide whether or not to strike. They are, left to right: Chris J. Golden, Philip Murray, John L. Lewis, John T. Dempsey, and Thomas Kennedy.

In the difficult years following World War I, as the union disintegrated under attack from the mine operators, Brophy became Lewis's major opponent. Brophy ran against Lewis as a matter of principle and on a real program—nationalization of the coal industry, organizing the unorganized, a labor party, democracy within the union, and labor education. The program made sense to the miners. But Lewis was a born ruler with little tolerance for dissent. He forced through UMW conventions constitutional amendments that gave him the power to appoint officers in the districts of the union. Formerly, such officers were elected by rank and file members. Brophy and many other miners were irked by Lewis's—and the UMW's—failure to provide financial support for local strikes and for strikers evicted from their company-owned homes.

Coal competition in the 1920's was cutthroat. The mine owners, operating at a three percent profit or less, were under tremendous pressure to cut the $7.50 day wages won under wartime contracts. Government ownership, or the kind of regulation provided later under the NRA, would have stabilized the industry—and, no doubt, saved the union. But

80

government ownership under the political climate generated by the "Return to Normalcy" under Harding, Coolidge, and Hoover was about as improbable as the formation of a labor party. This Lewis knew just as he knew that sporadic local strikes and indiscriminate strike relief would drain the union treasury. Saving the union also called for some centralizing of control, or so Lewis believed.

It took courage. At a UMW convention, a delegate, well known for his gun toting, rushed up to the platform to confront Lewis, who met him halfway and growled, "Take that gun out of your pocket or I'll shove it down your throat." The delegate hastily backed away. At another time, in the face of concerted howling by his opposition at a convention, Lewis boomed, "May the chair state that you may shout until you meet each other in hell and he will not change his ruling."

Courage was common among miners and Lewis's opposition possessed their share, too. Powers Hapgood, Harvard graduate, UMW organizer and a Brophy ally, would saunter along the barbed-wire entanglements and the armed guards posted outside non-union mines, calling out to the men on the way to work, "Don't scab, brothers. Join the United Mine Workers of America. We are on strike. Don't take the bread from your brothers' mouths. . . ." More often than not, he would be collared and run off to the nearest jail before he got too far. Hapgood, the son of a socially-minded Indianapolis businessman, was something of a puzzle to Lewis, who, according to McAllister Coleman, once sent for Hapgood and asked him what he was doing in the coalfields. "Organizing," said Hapgood. "Not writing a book?" queried Lewis.

History records that Lewis defeated Brophy in the 1926 election by a vote of 170,000 to 60,000. Brophy, however had the satisfaction of knowing that a substantial minority of the miners did favor his program. It was a remarkable achievement in that strife-torn union. "My campaign committee," Brophy wrote in his autobiography, "consisted, for the most part, of Powers Hapgood, Anita [Brophy's wife], and me, sitting around a table sending out the open letter [a statement of Brophy's platform]."

Lewis then drummed Brophy and Hapgood out of the mine union. After the founding of the CIO, Lewis brought both men back into the union, allowing them to hold membership cards as miners. However, they went to work for the CIO. It remains a sad thing that Brophy never again held an elective office. Lewis blocked a move to elect him secretary of the CIO, a post for which he was both eligible and eminently qualified. James B. Carey got the position instead from Lewis.

Typically, Brophy refused to allow his name to be put in nomination. For one thing, he did not have the support of his old union. (Lewis blocked that.) And, "I had no desire to be a storm center, especially when no issue or principle was involved." Moreover, Carey was a good choice "because it gave recognition to the younger generation." So, John Brophy stepped aside and served his beloved labor movement as director of organization of the CIO until his death in 1963 with a devotion beyond that of most leaders.

Brophy lacked that touch of iron that enabled Lewis to run roughshod over his opposition and to save the union at any cost. The 1920's was a time of trouble for the union. When a Congressional committee asked Richard B. Mellon, chairman of Pittsburgh Coal's Board of Directors from 1923 to 1925, about the machine guns in the hands of his coal and iron police, Mellon replied, "It is necessary. You cannot run the mines without them." The miner's $7.50 day was cut steadily until miners in Eastern Pennsylvania were earning $3 or $4 a day and weekly earnings of $6 to $10 were common in Northern fields where unemployment was a serious problem. The once proud UMW was down to a membership of 100,000 or less by 1933. Lewis's leadership appeared to be bankrupt.

VI. Sitdown!

When they tie the can to a union man,
  Sit down! Sit down!
When they give him the sack, they'll take him back,
  Sit down! Sit down!
Sit down, just take a seat,
Sit down, and rest your feet,
Sit down, you've got 'em beat.
  Sit down! Sit down!

The first "sit-down" strike according to writer Louis Adamic occurred at a most American event, a baseball game. Ball teams of union rubber workers sat down on the grass and refused to play until they were provided with an umpire who was a union man.

Later, during the winter of 1936, when Goodyear Tire and Rubber laid off 70 truck tire builders, the rubber workers remembered their spring training and sat down in the plant. This spontaneous action by 137 men led to mass picketing and a shut-down of the entire plant, involving 14,-000 workers. Under this pressure, the company quickly agreed to reconsider the firings. The company's prompt response was an eye-opener for rubber workers. During 1936 there was scarcely a week without at least one sit-down in a rubber plant, ranging in length from an hour or less to two or three days. Grievances, previously ignored by management, were given prompt attention.

The sit-down was an imaginative application of an old craft union technique to the industrial situation. The craftsmen's greatest source of strength was the ownership of the tools of his trade. When he had a grievance, or wished to strike for higher pay and better working conditions, he simply shut his tool box and carried it off the job. It was an exercise of his property right. Workers in the factory obviously could not carry off the tools with which they worked. But they could—and did for a time—sit down alongside, exercising their property rights in the job. "Sit Down!" asserted their right to a job with dignity.

The sit-down, too, was a rebellion against the dehumanization of the assembly line, the clamor of the factory. Ruth McKenney catches this in her book, *Industrial Valley,* where she gives a stunning description of the start of a sit-down in a tire factory. "The tirebuilders worked in a smooth frenzy," she wrote, "sweat around their necks, under their arms. The belt clattered, the insufferable racket and din and monotonous clash and uproar went on in steady rhythm." At a signal, one man yanked the master switch and the men stepped back from their machines, refusing to work.

"Instantly, the noise stopped. The whole room lay in perfect silence. The tirebuilders stood in long lines, touching each other, perfectly motionless, deafened by the silence. A moment ago there had been the weaving hands, the revolving wheels, the clanking belt, the moving hooks, the flashing tire tools. Now there was absolute stillness, no motion, no sound.

"Out of the terrifying quiet came the wondering voice of a big tirebuilder near the windows: . . . 'it's like the end of the world.'

"He broke the spell, the magic moment of stillness. For

now his awed words said the same thing to every man, 'We done it! We stopped the belt! . . . we done it!' And men began to cheer hysterically, to shout and howl in the fresh silence. Men wrapped long sinewy arms around their neighbors' shoulders, screaming, 'We done it! We done it!' "

The sit-down in the popular mind came to be associated with the CIO as a part of its style. But its use, in truth, became almost universal. Printers, pencil-makers, janitors, sailors, tobacco workers, bakers and candlestick makers, fishing tackle workers, Woolworth girls, rug weavers, restaurant and hotel employees, watchmakers, garbage collectors, newsstand clerks, dressmakers, farmhands, die casters and food-packers were among the countless variety of workers to catch the habit.

"You'd be sitting in the office any March day of 1937," Myra Wolfgang, an AF of L Hotel and Restaurant Employees' business agent recalled, "and the phone would ring and the voice at the other end would say, 'My name is Mary Jones; I'm a soda clerk at Liggett's; we've thrown the manager out and we've got the keys. What do we do now?' And you'd hurry over to the company to negotiate and over there they'd say, 'I think it's the height of irresponsibility to call a strike before you've ever asked for a contract,' and all you could answer was, 'You're so right.' "

Congress enacted the National Labor Relations Act on July 5, 1935. (The NRA was declared unconstitutional earlier that year.) The law, drafted by Senator Robert F.

Workers of Fisher Body Plant No. 3 of the General Motors Company at Flint, Michigan in a sit-down strike protesting the firing of several fellow workers in 1937.

Wagner of New York, guaranteed the right of workers to join organizations of their own choosing and the right to bargain collectively through their elected representatives. To give a bite to this basic policy decision, the Wagner Act created a new National Labor Relations Board (NLRB) empowered to order representation elections enabling workers to choose a union (or not choose a union) and to define and prohibit unfair labor practices (such as employer-dominated company unions, discriminatory discharge of union members, or the refusal on the part of employers to bargain in good faith).

The Wagner Labor Act was a protective umbrella over the workers' right to organize. The employers' successful use of blacklists and strikebreakers demonstrated that some government protection was essential if unions were to survive. The sit-downs were a test of the intentions of the Wagner Act—and of its effectiveness. From September, 1936, to May, 1937, sit-downs directly involved 484,711 workers.

In the end, the Supreme Court held that sit-downs were illegal. But by then (1939) their usefulness as a tactic had played out. The Court held the Wagner Act constitutional thereby assuring that workers discharged for union activity would be reinstated as a matter of law. This eliminated one of the chief causes of the major sit-downs. Moreover, the unions were on a more secure footing and workers began to air their grievances in the collective bargaining process. After all, it did not make sense to sit-down everytime a fellow worker had a beef against his foreman when he could take it to the union and get some corrective action. The time spent in settling grievances, incidentally, remains a major cause of wild-cat strikes where workers walk out while under contract and against the wishes of the union leadership.

The sit-downs, above all, were a response by the workers to their immediate situation. In November, 1936, as an instance, the organization of workers in the Fisher body plants of General Motors in Flint, Michigan, was going rather slowly. One evening, a number of workers signed application cards in a store-front meeting hall the union had rented across the street from Fisher. The next morning three welders, who had signed up, came to work only to find that their time cards had been lifted, which meant they were fired. Another union man protested to the foreman; he, too, was fired. As he was being paraded through the plant to the gate as an object lesson to the men at work, he passed Bud Simons, a torch solderer and union activist.

"Where are you going, Sam?" Simons asked.

"You come along, too, Bud," said the foreman.

Simons complied. But as he passed down the assembly line, each worker wiped his hands on his overalls and sat down. A hastily formed committee fell in behind Simons and the foreman. By the time they arrived at the front office, seven hundred men were idle. Simons noted the arrival of the committee at his back and turned to the plant manager.

"Mr. Parker," he said, "you are now talking to a union."

The sit-downers demanded that the discharged men be returned to their jobs and that everyone be paid for the time they had been sitting. The plant management quickly conceded and a lesson had been driven home. The power of union organization was too strong to be ignored by management.

"The CIO," Lewis declared, "stands for the punctilious observance of contracts, but we are not losing any sleep about strikes where employers refuse to recognize the well-defined principles of collective bargaining. A CIO contract is adequate protection for any employer against sit-downs, lie-downs, or any other kind of strike."

The spontaneity of the sit-down, however, would not have come to much if it had not been for the CIO. During the Atlantic City AF of L convention, John L. Lewis walked across a hotel lobby to tap Powers Hapgood on the shoulder. "I want to talk to you, Powers," he said to the organizer he

In 1939, members of the International Ladies' Garment Workers'Union presented a musical play called "Pins and Needles" that pleaded for labor peace. In a song "Papa Lewis and Mama Green," two members of the cast impersonate John L. Lewis and William Green.

had drummed out of the mine workers. "We're about to go into a campaign," he explained a few minutes later, "that will be everything you dreamed about and everything you've talked about. We're going out to fight for those things, and we're going to get them. You see, Powers, I've never really opposed these things. I just never felt that the time was ripe and that trying to do those things back in the days when we had our violent arguments would have been suicide for organized labor and would have resulted in complete failure. But now the time is ripe; and now the time to do these things is here. Let us do them."

"Lewis stopped talking," Hapgood later recalled, "and I just can't tell you how I felt. It was just as if everything I dreamed of had finally come to pass."

The day after the Atlantic City convention, Lewis met with Philip Murray, Thomas Kennedy, John Brophy of the Mine Workers, Charles P. Howard of the Typographical Workers, David Dubinsky of the International Ladies' Garment Workers' Union, Max Zaritsky of the Hat, Cap and Millinery Workers, and Thomas MacMahon of the Textile Workers. On November 9, they formed the Committee for Industrial Organizations, with the addition of Thomas Brown of the Mine, Mill and Smelter Workers and Harvey Fremming of the Oil Field, Gas Well and Refinery Workers. On November 23, 1935, Lewis wrote a terse note: "Effective this date, I resign as vice-president of the American Federation of Labor."

At the 1936 AF of L convention, Matthew Woll prepared a lengthy report condemning the "ingratitude" of the CIO unions. The executive council recommended suspension of the offenders. In March, 1937, William Green instructed city and state central bodies of the Federation to expel all delegates from the suspended ten CIO unions. The following year the Committee of Industrial Organizations became the Congress of Industrial Organizations. The split within the House of Labor was now complete.

Meanwhile, the CIO had experienced its first major strike. A cold winter blizzard hit Akron, the rubber capital of the world, on February 17, 1936. Two days before, Goodyear Tire & Rubber Company fired 137 workers without notice. Occasional sit-downs followed. On the 17th, a meeting of all employees was told that the company would not make any concessions. That night, workers in threadbare overcoats and belted mackinaws marched through the swirling snows on a straggling eleven-mile-long picket line. By the second day of the walkout, 10,000 were out on strike and the world's largest rubber factory was at a standstill.

The CIO sent Adolph Germer to direct the rubber workers organizing campaign. Powers Hapgood, Rose Pesotta, a New York dressmaker, Leo Krzycki of the Amalgamated

Clothing Workers, and John Schafer from the Oil Workers, came in to help Sherman Dalrymple, later president of the United Rubber Workers, and other local leaders run the strike.

The company retaliated with a charge that the strike was run by "outside agitators." The strikers explained that Goodyear profits for 1935 were a half-million dollars and that it paid its president $81,000 while proposing a layoff caused by lengthening the work day. "The two agitators in this strike are Goodyear hours and wages," a strike leader explained in a radio talk. "They are native products."

The rubber workers developed tactics that subsequently became characteristic of most CIO strikes. Pickets put up 68 tents and shanties, stringing them out along the eleven-mile picket line. Workers' wives organized a commissary that served 5,000 meals a day. Merchants donated $25,000 worth of food, clothing, and other supplies. Popular support for the strike was unquestionably strong. When six judges signed an injunction to restrain the mass picketing, another CIO trademark, no one could be found to serve the order, much less enforce it. The company demanded state troops but the governor refused to send any since, as the state labor movement quickly pointed out, there had been no violence to justify the use of the militia.

When a Law and Order League was formed and word went out that it would attack the picket line, the union leased the facilities of the local radio station. Strikers were instructed to keep tuned in all night. McAllister Coleman, a veteran socialist, union publicist, and newspaper reporter, directed an all-night program of entertainment, newscasts and strike bulletins. Union and civic leaders later credited this imaginative use of radio with forestalling bloodshed.

During the fourth week of the strike, Goodyear management finally agreed to meet with leaders of the union. Negotiations lasted another week and the strike ended on March 22, when a meeting of 5,000 workers met to hear the terms

1937 was a year of many strikes in various industries. Here textile strikers demonstrate in protest of the open shop. The employees later went on a sit-down strike.

of the settlement offer and voted their approval. The strikers won reinstatement of the discharged workers, a promise to notify workers of wage rate changes before they were put into effect, a reduction of hours and recognition of the union and union shop committees as spokesmen for its members.

In July, 1937, *Business Week* declared prophetically, "Akron is from nine months to a year ahead of the national procession in labor recovery. It was in Akron that the Committee for Industrial Organization made its first stand in a big industry. . . . Today all the big rubber companies in Akron are dealing across the table with unions."

Other industries, too, soon found the CIO a force to contend with, "When the Committee was formed two years ago its members did not total one million," John Brophy reported to the 1937 CIO convention. "Now there are four million." Aluminum workers, textile, electrical and newspaper workers, rapid transit, oil, shoe and shipyard workers and seamen rallied behind the banners of industrial unionism.

Employers greeted this uprising with something less than enthusiasm. In Maine, as an instance, shoe manufacturers retaliated against strikers with tear gas. Shoe town police broke up picket lines. Powers Hapgood, assigned to the shoeworkers at the time, spent six months in jail for his

91

defiance of a state court injunction barring union picketing. Employers, too, bought newspaper space to denounce trade unionists as "red radicals," revolutionaries seeking to overthrow law and order, business and the government.

In truth, however, the CIO was not as radical as all that. The aspirations of the mass production workers of the 1930's were much more modest than those of the workingmen's parties of the 1830's, the Knights of Labor, or of the Wobblies. Each of these sought to remake society according to some notion of what it *ought* to be. The workers of the 1930's wanted no more than recognition. (In 1937, 60 percent of all strikes were for union recognition. Unorganized workers are unrepresented and unprotected, their claims unheard or only distantly heard at the centers of power. The workingmen and working-women who made the rise of organized labor possible recognized that the giant corporations in auto, steel, rubber, and other mass production industries were here to stay. They did not want to destroy them. Sit-downers went out of their way to prevent damage to the plants they occupied. But they had grievances and they wanted to be heard.

"Labor does ask for and demand," thundered John L. Lewis, "a voice in the determination of those policies that affect the human element in industry. . . . It wants a place at the council table when decisions are made that affect the amount of food that the family of a worker may eat, the extent of education of his children, the kind and amount of clothing they shall wear, the few pleasures they may enjoy."

Before labor won this modest goal, however, many battles had to be fought. The way to the collective bargaining table was by marches on countless picket lines.

When strikes broke out in the auto industry, Lewis at first tried to head them off. He wanted to organize steel first. But the delegates who hitchhiked to South Bend, Indiana, and slept six and seven to a room to attend the auto workers' 1936 convention were not to be put off. They tossed out a

92

Thousands of these leaflets were distributed by the UAW at the Ford River Rouge Plant. It was the CIO's answer to cards handed out by Ford management bearing the title "Fordisms" and giving the company's alternatives to labor unions.

WIDE WORLD PHOTOS

leadership imposed by the AF of L and elected as president Homer Martin, an ex-Baptist minister from Saint Louis with a gift for agitation. Wyndham Mortimer, an ex-coal miner associated with the Communist Party faction in the union, was elected vice-president. George Addes, a shrewd, hard-headed Toledo Auto-Lite strike leader, was elected secretary-treasurer. Richard T. Frankensteen, a raucous, beefy ex-football tackle, brought the independent Chrysler workers' union into the United Automobile Workers after a brief struggle with the company. Walter P. Reuther, a fiery, red-headed socialist enlarged his growing West Side (Detroit) local by a five-day sit-down at the Kelsey-Hayes wheel plant. Lewis contributed $100,000 out of CIO funds to the UAW for organizing; in those days, it was a huge sum.

The chief target, of course, was General Motors, a combination of formerly independent automobile companies put together by the DuPonts and J. P. Morgan. Four hundred thousand men and women wrenched and hammered at cars and parts, putting things together as they moved along fast-paced assembly lines. The pace of work was set by white-shirted engineers with their time clocks. The workers had no say in this or other work practices in the auto plants. The myth that the industry paid well was assiduously cultivated by the auto companies. "In desperation," Clayton W. Fountain recalls in his autobiography, *Union Guy,* "I hit upon the scheme of going to Detroit to crash the gates of the automobile factories. In that city, according to the stories I had heard from workers who had worked in the auto plants, fabulous wages were paid in the shops that turned out millions of cars every year."

The Fountains of Detroit, however, were soon disillusioned. Seasonal layoffs for retooling and just plain layoffs shriveled income. In 1934, the annual earnings of half the auto workers was below a thousand dollars; that same year, GM's net profits were $167,000,000. The company and its executives did very well during the Depression. The average yearly wage was $1,150 in 1935, the same year GM president Alfred P. Sloan was paid $374,505 and vice-president William S. Knudsen, $325,868. GM's net profits in 1936 were $227,940,000. For the auto workers, there were no raises. And for this profitable industrial giant to refuse recognition to the auto workers' union was adding insult to injury.

In Flint, Michigan, 50,000 out of a total population of 165,000 toiled in GM's Chevrolet, Buick and Fisher body plants. GM's noted efficiency depended upon its network of specialized production plants. Each plant made essential parts which were then shipped to assembly lines where cars were put together. The union quickly realized that a shutdown of key production plants could halt the whole GM system. Though the workers' revolt against GM began in Georgia and spread to Kansas City and Cleveland, soon involving 140,000 GM workers, it finally centered on Flint, the heartland of the GM empire.

A National Guardsman with a "one pounder" cannon stands guard outside Chevrolet Plants No. 9 and No. 4 during strike at Flint, Michigan, 1937.

On January 11, 1937, while Governor Frank Murphy of Michigan sought to get negotiations moving, GM mounted a major attempt to force sit-downers out of Fisher Two, a key body plant. First, the heat, which had been maintained to protect the plant's water system, was shut off. Then the Flint police arrived and announced that no more food shipments would be allowed into the plant. A ladder placed to a window by the strikers was torn down by the police.

Strike leaders pleaded with the police to allow food to pass. Shortly after seven o'clock in the evening, pickets rushed the door, sweeping the police aside, and moved coffee and bread into the plant. Two hours later, fifty policemen, almost half of the Flint police force, attacked. They fired buckshot at the pickets outside and tear gas into the plant. The strikers fought back with soda-pop bottles, nuts and bolts, and two-pound steel automobile door hinges. Strikers captured four police cars. When the police massed for a final attack, the sit-downers hosed them back with powerful streams of cold water. Under the barrage of door hinges and torrents of water, the police retreated. The fight was over. GM gave up trying to evict sit-down strikers forcibly at Fisher Two and elsewhere. The rout of the police became a part of the

95

UAW's annals as the "Battle of the Running Bulls."

But the struggle with GM was far from over. Governor Frank Murphy sent some 1,500 National Guardmen to Flint to enforce peace of a kind. Murphy then prevailed upon the UAW to vacate the plants in return for a GM agreement to negotiate. On January 15, 1937, GM sit-downers left plants in Detroit and Anderson, Indiana. The Flint workers were due to vacate two days later.

A reporter, however, uncovered an exchange of telegrams between GM and the so-called Flint Alliance, a back-to-work movement sponsored by Flint businessmen. GM agreed, according to the telegram, to negotiate with the Alliance on an equal footing with the UAW. Considering this a betrayal of GM's committment to bargain collectively with their union, angry auto workers refused to leave the Flint plants.

The UAW, however, had not shut down Chevy Number Four, the motor-assembly division, nor Number Nine, a ball-bearing plant nearby. Since more pressure against the corporation seemed essential, a strategy meeting was held on the night of January 27. Roy Reuther the first organizer and first Reuther brother on the UAW payroll, Bob Travis UAW organizer and Flint strike leader, Powers Hapgood sent in to help by the CIO, and Kermit Johnson "Chevy" union leader, were the members of the committee. Reuther, who had a freshly-laundered shirt in his desk, drew out the cardboard and began sketching a battle plan. What was needed was a diversion, a move against Chevy Nine while a union task force captured the key Number Four plant. Secrecy was essential since company spies were plentiful. When the strike leaders proposed the seizure of Chevy Number Nine, the strikers set up derisive howls but in the end they were convinced.

On January 29, GM's plant guards were all mustered at Number Nine along with the Flint police. The UAW's women's auxiliary staged a demonstration in front of Plant Nine. Victor Reuther was in the street with his sound truck; Walter was on hand with reinforcements from the Kelsey-

Hayes wheel plant. For over a half-hour, a fierce battle raged outside Plant Nine. Tear gas brought tears to strikers' eyes. Windows were broken. The police and strikers exchanged bloody blows.

Then there was a sudden silence at Chevy Four. As the weary demonstrators marched from Chevy Nine to rally outside Chevy Four, strikers perched on the roof of Four began to sing,

> When the union's inspiration through the
> workers' blood shall run,
> There can be no power greater anywhere
> beneath the sun.
> Yet what force on earth is weaker than
> the feeble strength of one?
> But the union makes us strong.

And, back from the streets came the chorus:

> Solidarity forever!
> Solidarity forever!
> Solidarity forever!
> For the Union makes us strong.

The seizure of Number Four meant the end of the strike. Governor Murphy, furious, threatened to oust the strikers by force. Lewis replied, "I do not doubt your ability to call out your soldiers and shoot the members of our union out of those plants, but let me say when you issue that order I shall leave this conference and I shall enter one of those plants with my people."

President Roosevelt requested GM to meet with the union. Lewis insisted that GM give the UAW exclusive bargaining rights. The company finally capitulated on February 11 and agreed, at Governor Murphy's suggestion, to recognize and deal with the UAW for the 17 plants closed by strikes. The union had won a significant victory. In a few weeks, the UAW doubled its membership, from 100,000 to 200,000.

VII. Big Steel...Little Steel

LATE IN THE AFTERNOON OF March 1, 1937, Philip Murray, the director of the CIO's Steel Workers' Organizing Committee, answered a telephone call from a steel organizer in Aliquippa, Pennsylvania.

"One of the steel workers just came in and said he heard over the radio that U.S. Steel was meeting with the CIO," the organizer said. "I told him he was crazy and kicked him out of the office."

"Well," said Murray, "you'd better apologize. It's true."

The organizer from Aliquippa wasn't the only one surprised. It is said that Benjamin Fairless, the president of U.S. Steel, did not know of the pending agreement, between John L. Lewis and Myron C. Taylor, chairman of U.S. Steel Board of Directors, until the day before it was signed on March 2, 1937.

When the Steel Workers' Organizing Committee launched its drive to organize the industry on June 13, 1936, everyone expected a head-breaking conflict. The American Iron and Steel Institute placed a full page advertisement in 375 daily newspapers at a cost of a half-million dollars announcing the steel industry's opposition to the SWOC drive. The newspaper salvo was backed by a stepped-up industry drive to

98

organize company unions under a so-called "employee representation plan." U.S. Steel, for example, spent $75,000 a year to support "employee representation" in a single mill. The Institute's advertisement, cried Lewis, "is a declaration of war."

The first skirmish was a matter of statistics with the union drawing first blood. The Iron and Steel Institute contended that the steel industry paid higher wages than any other industry in the country. Nonsense, asserted Lewis. Hourly wages in March, 1936, were 65.6 cents in steel, 79.3 cents in bituminous coal, 83.2 in hard coal, and 79.8 in building construction. (The latter three were unionized rates.) Common labor in steel, said Lewis, received 47.9 cents an hour and for that work the steel industry rated twentieth place in a list of twenty-one major industries.

The advertisement actually backfired for it provided far greater publicity for the SWOC than it could muster on its own. CIO became a by-word in the mills before the steel union organizers even arrived. The company hopes of forestalling the union through employee representation plans also came to nothing. CIO activists simply joined the plans, gave them a shot of militancy, and converted company unions into steel union locals. U.S. Steel, in a sense, "organized" its own employees for the CIO.

In the end, however, the unionization of U.S. Steel was a Lewis triumph. Many lives had been lost—at Homestead and during the 1919 strike—in the battle for union recognition. Now the chief bastion of the open shop fell without so much as a solitary picket. The United Auto Workers agreement with General Motors had been reached a week earlier as a result of a long and bitter sit-down strike. The Lewis-Taylor agreement avoided that kind of high-cost settlement. U.S. Steel recognized SWOC as the collective bargaining agent for its members, agreed to an increase in the daily minimum wage to $5 and to a five-day, forty-hour week with time-and-a-half for overtime.

Lewis's success stimulated countless rumors explaining

99

U.S. Steel's about-face and acceptance of the CIO. According to one story, Taylor happened to be dining with his wife at the same Washington restaurant as Lewis in December, 1936, and Mrs. Taylor noticed the CIO chief and said to her husband, "Myron, I want to meet that man. Bring him over here." Taylor did so and friendship ripened in the SWOC-U.S. Steel agreement.

But there was more to that historic agreement than a casual social meeting in a Washington restaurant. Taylor was much more reconciled to the New Deal than his executive colleagues in the steel industry. He also benefited from the advice of Tom Moses, president of the U.S. Steel subsidiary H.S. Frick Coal Company, who had negotiated with Lewis and enjoyed a friendly relationship with the CIO leader.

Still, though personalities may have helped smooth the way for an agreement, business considerations carried the day. U.S. Steel's decision to bargain collectively with SWOC was based on a hard-headed assessment of current economic and political conditions. SWOC had signed up a majority of the employees at Carnegie-Illinois and other U.S. Steel plants. The steel workers were in a militant mood and the GM strike made it abundantly clear that the cost of open conflict with the CIO came high both in terms of money and public opinion. A Senate investigating committee, chaired by Senator LaFollette, indicated that it would look into the labor espionage practices of the corporation.

Outweighing even these hefty considerations, however, was the presence in the United States of Lord Runciman, president of the British Board of Trade, who was arranging for the purchase of steel for Great Britain's rearmament program. Before letting contracts, Lord Runciman wanted assurances of uninterrupted production. This decided Thomas W. Lamont in favor of collective bargaining in steel. Lamont was a partner in J. P. Morgan and Company and the key man on the powerful finance committee of U.S. Steel's Board of

100

A home overlooking the steel works of Carnegie Illinois Steel Corporation Plant at Braddock, Pennsylvania.

Directors. He realized that only through union recognition could the corporation avoid labor conflict and break-downs in production. Once Lamont was decided, the rest was a foregone conclusion.

For a time, it seemed likely that the balance of the steel industry would follow suit. On April 12, the U.S. Supreme Court upheld the constitutionality of the Wagner Labor Act. It backed a National Labor Relations Board decision that called for the reinstatement of a number of Jones & Laughlin employees fired for union activity. The company, then in negotiations with SWOC, however, balked at signing a contract. The union called a strike and 36 hours later J&L capitulated. The company agreed to "exclusive recognition"— a step beyond U.S. Steel's "members only"—if a majority of its employees voted for the proposal in an NLRB election. This they did, two to one, on May 20, and the Steel Workers became the sole bargaining agent for all J&L's blue collar work force. That month, Phillip Murray announced that SWOC had 325,000 members and contracts with 90 companies, including all the subsidiaries of U.S. Steel, and key independents such as Wheeling Steel, Timkin Roller Bearings, Caterpillar Tractor, and McKeesport Tin-Plate. SWOC was on the march.

But there were signs of trouble ahead. Republic Steel fired 75 workers for union activity and shut down its Massillon

101

plant, a SWOC stronghold. This opening gun in an all-out struggle was fired by Tom M. Girdler, president of Republic Steel and a rugged corporate individualist who hated unions. He rallied the so-called "Little Steel" companies—Republic, Bethlehem, Inland, and Youngstown Sheet & Tube Corporation—to do battle with the steel union. In the Little Steel effort to destroy SWOC, Girdler applied ruthlessly the Mohawk Valley Formula, which consisted of tactics devised by James H. Rand, Jr., to combat the International Association of Machinists during the 1936 Remington Rand strikes. The Formula was widely publicized by the National Association of Manufacturers and has served as the text for anti-union tactics ever since. The ingredients of the formula are deceptively simple: The plan of attack calls for an employer-conducted strike ballot; the labeling of union leaders as "outside agitators," "communists," and "radicals"; economic pressure on the community by threats to move plants; the organization of a back-to-work movement to cover up the employment of strikebreakers; a show of police and "Citizens' Committee" force; and a grandstand opening of struck plants.

Following Girdler's lead, the Little Steel companies rejected all SWOC overtures for negotiations. On May 26, a strike against Little Steel was called by the union. By June 1, 70,000 workers were out on strike in seven states and a dozen cities in an effort to shut down Little Steel.

On May 30, 1937, white clouds scudded across the blue sky above Sam's Place, where the strikers from Republic Steel's South Chicago plant gathered to hear speakers. Whole families came in their Sunday best. The Republic plant lay to the South across a field and some railroad tracks.

During the meeting, a statement from the mayor affirming the workers' rights to picket peacefully was read to the crowd. Someone proposed that the strikers go over and picket the Republic plant to assert that right. A motion was made and passed.

102

Casually, the strikers with their families strolled by twos and threes and in small groups towards the plant.

Later, in an effort to discover what happened, the LaFollette Senate Committee held intensive hearings. A Paramount news film showed a leader of the strikers arguing quietly with the police. He insisted that the strikers had the right to picket peacefully. Other strikers joined in to argue with the police. Suddenly, shots rang out. "The first shots came from the police," concluded the LaFollette Committee, "unprovoked." In seconds, the orderly, strolling crowd was in shambles. The motion picture film shows workers in full flight, many stumbling along with hands upraised.

Some strikers retaliated with stones or whatever else came to hand from the field. But most fled in terror. Ten were shot, seven in the back, three in the side, none in front. Thirty others were so badly beaten that they required hospitalization, and some 30 more received injuries requiring medical treatment. The police reported 35 of their men injured, none were shot and only three required hospitalization.

Striker Earl Handley was shot. Workers got him into a car, hoping to get him medical aid. But the police dragged him out and he bled to death.

Sam Popovich fled from the flailing clubs. He stumbled and fell. The police beat him while he was down and he died, an old man with his bald head battered in by police clubs.

"The police," noted the LaFollette Committee report, "dragged seriously wounded, unconscious men along the ground with no more care than would be employed on a common drunkard."

Mrs. Lupe Marshall, a ninety-two pound, four-foot eleven-inch social worker and mother of three children, tried to help the wounded. She was clubbed around the head by police. In the Paramount film, you can see a policeman, twice her size, viciously twist her around and shove her into the patrol wagon.

Inside were sixteen dying or seriously wounded strikers. Mrs. Marshall did her best to lift them off one another, to sort out the pile of injured humanity. The floor was bloody and slippery underneath. But Mrs. Marshall finally pillowed one man's bloody head in her lap. As the wagon bounced through Chicago streets, he gestured for a cigarette. Mrs. Marshall searched his pockets and found a useless packet soaked with blood.

"Never mind, you're a good kid," he told Mrs. Marshall, then shivered and died.

At the hospital, there were calls from the doctors and nurses for volunteers to help with the wounded. But the police drove the volunteers away. Mrs. Marshall tried to comfort a wounded, scared little boy. The police shoved her away. Her head finally bandaged, she felt woozy and went to the ladies' rest room. A policeman followed her, grabbed her arm. "I guess you can walk all right." She was dragged out of the hospital and off to jail.

The St. Louis *Post Dispatch* was the first newspaper to carry an account of the Paramount newsfilm, which was not shown "for fear of inciting riots throughout the country." The account ends as follows:

Police hold back sympathizers at the Republic Steel Plant in Chicago on May 30, 1937. The picture is from a newsreel that had been banned "for fear of inciting riots throughout the country."

"There is continuous talking, but it is difficult to distinguish anything, with one exception—out of the babble there rises this clear and distinct ejaculation:

" 'God Almighty!'

"The camera shifts back to the central scene. Here and there is a body sprawled in what appears to be the grotesque indifference of death. Far off toward the outer corner of the field, whence they had come originally, the routed marchers are still in flight, with an irregular line of policemen in close pursuit. It is impossible to discern, at this distance, whether violence has ended.

"A policeman, somewhat disheveled, his coat open, a scowl on his face, approaches another who is standing in front of the camera. He is sweaty and tired. He says something indistinguishable. Then his face breaks into a sudden grin, he makes a motion of dusting off his hands, and strides away. The film ends."

What became known in labor history as the Memorial Day Massacre, however, was only a beginning. In Massillon, Ohio, a Republic Steel official demanded of Chief of Police Stanley Switter: "Why don't you take action like they did in Chicago?" Switter later told the National Labor Relations Board

Using guns, clubs and tear gas, police battle Republic Steel Company strikers and their sympathizers during the demonstration that came to be known as the "Memorial Day Massacre."

that company officials and members of the Law and Order League "put the heat on" until guns were placed in the hands of "special police." Switter was persuaded to leave town—how isn't exactly clear but leave he did—and the "specials" under other leaders provoked a riot in which two strikers were killed and several wounded. Before the riot ended, 160 strikers were arrested.

In Johnstown, Pennsylvania, Mayor Daniel J. Shields headed up the local back-to-work committee. He issued tin hats and gave permission to carry clubs to supervisory employees of Bethlehem Steel. The Mayor would turn up at picket lines and order the pickets to move on, directing the arrest of those who moved too slowly to suit him. Then, he would sit on the magistrate's bench to try strike cases. Mayor

Wounded strikers huddled together on the ground after police took control of the Republic Steel strikers' demonstration.

Shields received $31,456 from Bethlehem Steel which was to be paid to deputy sheriffs employed during the strike.

In Cleveland, Ohio, a strikebreaker's car crushed a striker to death against an iron fence. A mob wrecked strike headquarters. In Canton, Ohio, nervous troopers drove derisive children from playgrounds at bayonet point. Three youngsters, all under sixteen, bled so badly they had to be treated in the medical corps room at the Canton armory. The press was asked "to cooperate" by suppressing the incident.

The CIO looked to President Roosevelt for help. After all, hadn't they contributed much to the landslide victory of 1936 when Roosevelt carried all but two states? Roosevelt, as Arthur M. Schlesinger, Jr., puts it in his monumental *Age of Roosevelt, The Coming of the New Deal,* "viewed both sides with detachment." He also lacked real empathy for trade unionism. "Reared in the somewhat paternalistic traditions of pre-war progressivism and of the social work ethos," writes Schlesinger, "Roosevelt thought instinctively in terms of the government's doing things for working people rather than of giving the unions power to win workers their own victories."

By 1937, Roosevelt had secured the enactment of his New Deal program, much of which favored working people. Still, workers insisted on organizing and instead of the domestic peace he expected, Roosevelt's second term began at a time of deepening labor-management strife. Irritated by this, Roosevelt snapped out a quote from Shakespeare: "A plague on both your houses." John L. Lewis parried with a weak quip, "Which house, Hearst or Du Pont?" The newspaper magnate, Hearst, was a virulent critic of the President and the DuPonts had heavy financial interests in the then turbulent auto industry.

The Presidential rebuff came at a time when organized labor needed support. Lewis, understandably, was angry; the Rooseveltian rebuke would rankle him until the President's death in 1945. A sorely wounded lion, Lewis rumbled

WIDE WORLD PHOTOS

A non-striking worker is attacked and beaten by strikers after leaving the Corrigan-McKinney Plant of Republic Steel Corporation in Cleveland, Ohio.

over a coast-to-coast radio hookup: "Labor, like Israel, has many sorrows. Its women weep for their fallen and they lament for the future of the children of the race. It ill behooves one who has supped at labor's table and who has been sheltered in labor's house to curse with equal fervor and fine impartiality both labor and its adversaries when they become locked in deadly embrace."

The strikes against Bethlehem and Youngstown Sheet & Tube were lost; the blow was softened somewhat by an agreement with Inland Steel patterned upon the U.S. Steel agreement and secured through the mediation efforts of Governor Townsend of Indiana. The effects of the Little Steel strike lasted as late as 1945 when Republic paid $350,-000 to settle suits brought against the company on behalf

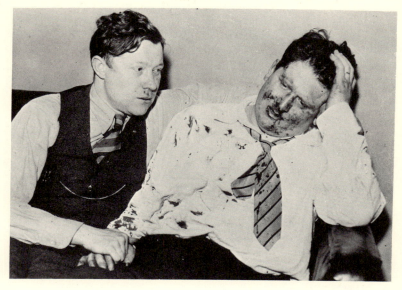

Walter Reuther (left) with Richard Frankensteen after they had been battered by Ford security men for handing out union circulars at the plant in Dearborn.

of strikers who had been killed or injured. Eventually, 7,000 strikers were reinstated by the NLRB with back pay rewards amounting to two million dollars.

Still, the Little Steel defeats of 1937 rankled. It was a bad year for organized labor. During the spring, the UAW moved on Ford's giant River Rouge plant. The auto workers had permits from the city of Dearbon to distribute handbills. The unionists went to the overpass across Miller Road at Gate Four where they were met by Ford "servicemen," or private guards. Ordered off Ford property, the union men turned to leave. They were jumped by fifty of Ford's hirelings. William Merriweather, an auto worker who had volunteered to pass out leaflets, was knocked down as the Ford men shouted, "Kill him, kick his brains out, stomp his face in."

109

They broke his back. Ralph Dunham and Tony Marinovich suffered crippling head injuries as a result of beatings at the hands of the Ford guards. Another group of service men attacked some UAW women getting off a street car, twisted their arms and called them foul names. One girl was kicked in the stomach.

Back at the overpass, the Ford men grabbed UAW vice-president Richard Frankensteen and Walter Reuther. Both were badly beaten. Reuther later testified before an NLRB hearing: "Seven times they raised me off the concrete and threw me down on it. They pinned my arms and shot short jabs to my face. I was punched and dragged by my feet to the stairway. I grabbed the railing and they wrenched me loose. I was thrown down the first flight of steps until I found myself on the ground where I was beaten and kicked."

Henry Ford was determined to whip the union. He was a strong-willed man who ran his company with a velvet-gloved iron hand. He hired Harry Bennett, an ex-sailor and former boxer, to head his private police, the famous Ford Servicemen. Bennett, incidentally, wrote a book about his experiences with Ford with the marvelous title, *We Never Called Him Henry*. Ford paid well but he was a stern task-master, an attitude he carried over to the policing of the private lives of his employees. Bennett's men were not only expected to police the grounds, nose into production standards and keep union men away but they were also expected to pry into the off-the-job lives of Ford employees. Ford, for example, was a teetotaler and he insisted that Bennett's staff check out the drinking habits of Ford employees.

Ford, however, was a charitable man. He contributed heavily to the churches—and their charities—of his employees. He was often generous though fickle. Bennett tells of a gift of a car to a Ford executive who had pleased his employer. A short time later, however, he fell out of favor, and Ford sent one of Bennett's men over to take the car away, out of the man's driveway, without notifying him, or for that matter, ever telling him what he had done.

110

Paternalism of Ford's sort often provided the cement that held an enterprise together as it grew from small beginnings to giant size. But when employees become too many for the employer to know individually, paternalism is frequently reinforced by the services of the Harry Bennetts. Employees were spied upon. Any man caught talking union was fired. Ministers were pressured into preaching against unionism. The union faced a long, hard struggle when it came to organizing Ford.

At Republic Steel the strike straggled on. A handful of wary and weary pickets marched before Republic plant gates, resting in-between turns in a tent set up nearby. One dark night in Niles, Ohio, the flood lights at the Republic Plant were switched off. Suddenly, a bundle of gasoline-saturated rags was hurled, flaming, into the pickets' tent. Luckily, no one was hurt. But everything was destroyed—an electric refrigerator, a radio, stove, coffee-urn, tables, dishes, and food—all the makings of a long seige at the gates crumbled into ashes and twisted bits of metal.

VIII. How Much Production…, Mr. Hook?

HITLER'S TANKS ROLLED ACROSS the face of Europe in 1940, starting the Second World War. A worried American President urged the building of an "arsenal for democracy." Walter P. Reuther suggested that the idle facilities of the automobile industry be used to produce an estimated 500 planes a day. The AF of L demanded full representation for labor on all governmental defense agencies. Philip Murray proposed the creation of industry councils for each major defense industry. These would consist of an equal number of labor and management representatives with a government official to coordinate production, train workers and promote industrial peace.

Yet, on the eve of Pearl Harbor there were still some seven million jobless in the United States. The year before December 7, 1941, had been an uneasy one. The number of strikes swelled to a peak higher than in any previous year, except 1917 and 1927. During 1941, more than 4,200 strikes involving over 2.3 million workers caused a loss to industry of 23,000,000 man-days. Crucial defense plants were affected. Allis-Chalmers, a manufacturer of farm machinery, was shut down for 76 days in the spring. A strike halted fighter airplane pro-

112

duction at the Inglewood, California, plant of North American Aviation, Inc. The President sent troops to seize and re-open the plant on June 9.

Much of the labor turmoil of that year was left-over business from the late 1930's. The UAW, for example, resumed its campaign to organize Ford in the winter of 1940-41. In February, the Supreme Court refused a Ford request to review an NLRB order for the reinstatement of 22 River Rouge workers fired for union activity. The reinstated men returned to their jobs wearing UAW buttons. It was the first time that any Ford workers dared to display pro-union sentiment openly. Others joined the union and a rash of sit-downs broke out over long-standing grievances.

On April 1, 1941, Ford fired the whole eight-man UAW grievance committee at the River Rouge plant. Without any order from the union, Ford workers downed their tools. At the end of the day, the largest single auto plant in the world was shut down tight. On the first full day of the strike, the union, which set up a field headquarters manned by eight doctors and six nurses, reported that 150 persons were given medical aid as a result of violence.

Much to everyone's surprise, Ford agreed next day not to work on the River Rouge plant. Violence was virtually non-existent thereafter. Intensive negotiations settled the strike in ten days with Ford's agreement to an NLRB representation election. On May 21, 1941, the UAW won 51,866 to the AF of L's 20,364 and 1,958 "neither" votes. Ford then became the first major manufacturer to grant a union shop and the check-off of union dues.

Ford, according to Harry Bennett, head of the auto company's security department, rather liked the idea of the check-off. He told Bennett, "That will make us their bankers, won't it? Then they can't get along without us. They'll need us just as bad as we need them."

It was shrewd industrial relations psychology. But it was not the full explanation of the Ford turn-around. After all,

Early in the 1940's strikes halted production in many defense plants. Police used fire hoses along with tear gas shells to quell strikers at the Allis Chalmers Plant in Milwaukee.

Henry Ford had once announced "we'll never recognize the United Automobile Workers or any other union." Also Ford had administered a major union defeat in 1937 and succeeded in fending off union organizational efforts ever since.

Ford gave in—as did the Little Steel companies—because of the threat of war. Defense plans were well under way and their success depended upon uninterrupted production. The labor turmoil of 1941 showed what dissatisfied workers could do to upset steady output. Moreover, organized labor possessed enough political power to pressure Washington against the awarding of valuable defense contracts to non-union firms. For instance, in January, 1941, just before the successful UAW strike at Ford, a large contract for Army trucks by-passed Ford Motor Company. It was exactly the kind of deal that would alert Henry Ford to labor's rising power.

The approach of war—and the war itself—also affected the rivalry between the AF of L and the CIO. The latter so captured public imagination—and wrought such a great change in the mass production industries—that we forget that the split of the CIO actually had a liberating effect on

114

the AF of L. The Federation entered the mid-thirties crusty, craft-ridden and just plain suspicious of the appeals for organization from the auto, rubber, and steel centers. The AF of L's old guard scorned government intervention quite as much as the most conservative businessmen. They believed that workers could rely only on their own organizational strength to resist the pressure of employers, avoid being tripped up by a change of administrations, and survive economic adversity. In the light of labor history, this made some sense, but it failed to take into account the real underlying changes in the United States that accepted the unions as a counter power to big business.

The break away of the CIO and the enactment of the Wagner Act changed the AF of L. After the split, the Federation responded with a vigor that nearly surpassed its new rival, the CIO. It, too, took advantage of the new governmental machinery set up to assist collective bargaining. During the last four months of 1936, the AF of L payroll for organizers was $82,000; in the last four months of 1937, it was $466,000. In 1937, the AF of L had a membership of 2.8 million; the CIO, 1.5 million. By 1941, the AF of L had a membership of 4.5 million to the CIO's 2.8 million. Membership in the CIO jumped during the war years to over 5 million but the AF of L membership remained larger, closer to 6 million. However, the change was such that the CIO retained its glamor in the public eye. It also held a political edge because of its greater committment to political action. The Federation, at the time, was not as deeply involved in the support of pro-labor candidates as it and the AFL-CIO later became. This political advantage bore fruit in the Presidential appointment of Sidney Hillman, president of the Amalgamated Clothing Workers and vice-president of the CIO, as an associate director of the Office of Production Management under William S. Knudsen, formerly of General Motors.

In the Presidential view, Hillman's appointment signalled a wartime labor-management partnership. But it wasn't enough of an appointment, nor a sufficient recognition of organized labor to suit John L. Lewis. And Lewis's formidable burly figure did loom over the wartime labor scene despite a sudden change in his circumstances as a leader of labor.

Still bitter in 1940 at the rebuke administered the unions by Roosevelt in 1937, Lewis came out against Roosevelt's re-election for a third term. He did so in a particularly dramatic fashion, over the radio in a last minute election eve appeal to American workers. "Sustain me now or repudiate me," Lewis declared, pledging that he would quit as president of the CIO if Roosevelt were re-elected. Neither his coal miners nor the members of the CIO heeded his call to desert Roosevelt for Republican candidate Wendell Wilkie. So, Lewis stepped down as president of the CIO on November 18, 1940.

Nonetheless, Lewis maintained a great hold on the CIO. He remained, as always, president of the United Mine Workers, still a powerful union. The CIO owed too great a debt to Lewis and the UMW to cast them off lightly. His personal influence over the leaders of the CIO was tremendous; *they* had not wanted him to step down. Moreover, they were not too happy at any prospect that might involve Lewis's return to the AF of L.

Sidney Hillman, however, who had supported Roosevelt in 1940, was willing to try to trim the lion's mane. He negotiated an exclusive agreement with the AF of L building trades on behalf of defense agencies. This agreement froze out the CIO's struggling construction union, headed by Lewis's brother, Denny, from any share in defense construction. When Hitler attacked Russia, on June 23, 1941, the Communists, then an important group within the CIO, deserted Lewis, who was against American involvement in the war, for Hillman. So, Lewis's hold over the CIO was weakened but not so much as his enemies may have desired.

Lewis, morever, had great recuperative powers as a leader.

116

All the unions feared a wartime loss of membership under a government labor policy that would set wages and working conditions instead of leaving such matters to the free play of collective bargaining. Lewis, who shared this fear, demanded a union shop for his members in the "captive" mines owned by the steel companies. The union shop would guarantee that all employees must become and remain union members for the duration of a collective bargaining agreement. This was opposed by the steel companies. They realized that it would affect the steel mills where the Steel Workers Union still represented members only.

After a mine shutdown of two days in late October, the dispute was referred to the National Defense Mediation Board. On November 10, the Board voted nine to two to reject the UMW demand. Murray and Thomas Kennedy, ex-miners who voted nay, resigned. That ended the usefulness of the Board though it did not dispose of the issue. Lewis ordered a strike of the miners in the captive anthracite mines. Eleven striking pickets were shot and wounded at the Frick coke plant at Edenborn, Pennsylvania. Lewis was denounced for blocking the defense effort despite the truth of Lewis's rebuttal: "Defense output is not impaired and will not be impaired for an indefinite period."

In this Pulitzer Prize-winning photograph, strikers gang up on an anti-union man outside the Ford Plant at River Rouge, Michigan, on April 3, 1941.

WIDE WORLD PHOTOS

Sidney Hillman (right) and John L. Lewis at 1936 AF of L convention.

Still, the nation could not very well tolerate a coal strike at this critical time nor could it authorize the bloody suppression of the miners. Congress had just authorized the arming of merchant vessels. Japanese envoys were carrying on discussions in Washington. On November 22, Lewis accepted a White House proposal that the captive-mines dispute be arbitrated by a board consisting of Benjamin F. Fairless, president of U.S. Steel; John R. Steelman, director of the U.S. Conciliation Service; and Lewis. The miners went back to work and Lewis, confident that Steelman would see the issue his way, met with his fellow arbitrators. The board's vote was two to one for the union shop in the captive mines but its significance was lost in the day's headlines. It was December 7, 1941, the day Japan bombed Pearl Harbor and forced the United States into World War II.

The significance of the decision, however, was not lost on the leaders of the AF of L or the CIO. Lewis had pulled a major coup. At a conference of labor and management summoned by the President to work out settlement of wartime labor disputes, Lewis emerged as the leader of all organized labor. The conferees quickly agreed that there should be no strikes or lockouts for the duration of the war. But they deadlocked on the issue of union security, some guarantee of continued union membership and influence. The industry representatives argued for the *status quo*. The trade unionists insisted that a proposed wartime

118

mediation board be empowered to grant a union or a closed shop in plants where the open shop prevailed at the outbreak of the war. When industrialist Charles R. Hook pleaded for the open shop, Lewis retorted: "I have heard this open shop talk before. The open shop is a harlot with a wig and artificial limbs, and her bones rattle. But how much production will she give us, Mr. Hook?"

It appeared likely that Lewis would secure an agreement on the union shop, a victory that would have made him the undisputed spokesman for American labor. But President Roosevelt cut the conference short, forestalling a Lewis success. The President accepted the proposed ban on wartime strikes and lockouts and declared that he would create a war labor board that would "cover of necessity all disputes that may arise between labor and management," including the union security issue. William H. Davis, a former patent attorney and chairman of the now-abandoned National Defense Mediation Board, was named chairman of the new agency created by executive order on January 12, 1942.

The union security issue was to be fought out on a case-by-case basis before the new War Labor Board. However, the Board soon worked out a basic policy for handling such cases. It provided the individual employee with an escape period of 15 days after the signing of a labor contract, during which he could withdraw from the union for the duration of the contract. If he failed to exercise the option, he had to stay a member. "By and large," reasoned a WLB majority in the key Caterpillar Tractor case, "the maintenance of a stable union membership makes for the maintenance of responsible union leadership and responsible union discipline makes for keeping faithfully the terms of the contract and provides a stable basis for union-management cooperation for more efficient production."

Sophisticated management learned during the war, thanks to the maintenance of membership policy by the WLB, that collective bargaining could be an effective way of working

Sign hung in front of John L. Lewis' UMW headquarters to remind CIO chief of his promise to resign if President Roosevelt were elected for a third term.

out personnel problems within corporate structures that were too unwieldy for the old-fashioned employer-employee face-to-face relationship to work with equity or satisfaction. Collective bargaining, in this light, became a system for drawing up the rules for employment; grievance procedures, a way of resolving on-the-job conflicts; and the unions became agencies for enforcing the rules.

The usefulness of the unions in this new role was driven home by wartime experience. Industry was confronted by a sudden influx of new workers. Some were unruly, ready to strike at the slightest grievance. Many unions during the war took disciplinary action against leaders of wildcats, that is, unauthorized strikes. Labor's success in this new role may be judged by the record. In 1942, only five one-hundredths of one percent of war work was delayed because of strikes. "That record," declared President Roosevelt, "has never been equaled in this country. It is as good or better than the record of any of our allies in wartime."

Though John L. Lewis had been neatly sidetracked by the President, he was still a force to be reckoned with. Two former Lewis aides—Green and Murray—headed the two wings of the labor movement. The American people were united in the war effort and the time seemed ripe for unifying the labor movement. And John L. Lewis appeared to be the man for the job.

On January 17, 1942, Lewis, as chairman of the CIO negotiations committee, sent a letter to Green and Murray suggesting the resumption of peace talks between the AF of L and the CIO. Always arrogant, Lewis did not bother to inform Philip Murray, who had replaced him as president of the CIO, of the move. He had, however, caucused with the two most powerful men in the AF of L—William Hutcheson of the Carpenters and Dan Tobin of the Teamsters. According to A. H. Raskin of *The New York Times,* an agreement had been reached. Green was to retire; AF of L secretary-treasurer George Meany was slated to be president of the united movement. Lewis would represent the CIO as first or second vice-president on an expanded executive council. Murray was to be named secretary-treasurer. Green immediately accepted the Lewis invitation to the peace talks. Murray, who first read about the letter in the newspapers, retorted, "No one has the right to trade me for a job." Angrily, he declared that any unity move would have to start through his office.

Aside from any desires of Lewis's, the impulse for unity stemmed from labor's need to speak with a single voice in wartime councils on an equal basis with industry. President Roosevelt, always politically adroit, intervened by forming a "labor cabinet" of three AF of L and three CIO leaders. This Labor Victory Board met from time to time

With many men gone to war, women became the vital "manpower" of the defense industry.

at the White House and served to fend off Lewis's efforts at unifying the AF of L and CIO.

Frustrated, Lewis pulled his mine union out of the CIO. Later, he would re-enter the AF of L only to leave after a time to go it alone. His failure to put together the house he had put asunder was a sad climax to his career as the dominant figure in the American labor movement.

Nonetheless, Lewis was destined to be the central figure in the major World War II labor conflict, the wartime 1943 coal strike.

The strike had its origins in the government's wartime

Harlan, Kentucky miners read their local newspaper for details of President Roosevelt's back-to-work order in 1943.

wage and price policy. The Stabilization Act of 1942 authorized the President to stabilize wages and salaries at September, 1942, levels. As a result of NLRB representation elections, the Little Steel companies agreed to recognize the steel union as bargaining agent but they balked at the union's wage demands in negotiations. As a result of numerous delays, the wage question was put into the lap of the War Labor Board.

The Board found, after much deliberation, that there had been a 15 percent rise in the cost of living between 1941, and 1942. It held, therefore, that the steel workers were entitled to a raise to compensate for the difference despite the federal ban on new wage increases. The so-called Little Steel Formula was applied to other situations calling for similar wage adjustments.

However, prices were also allowed to rise, putting a strain on the Little Steel Formula. Moreover, workers found employers using the WLB procedures as a way of postponing the settlement of grievances. By 1943, there was a backlog of 17,000 undecided cases before the Board. To many trade unionists, it seemed that "fighting a war" had become an excuse to postpone the correction of some wrongs.

The soft coal miners, who had already received their full allotment under the Little Steel formula, demanded an increase of two dollars a day, vacation benefits and "portal-to-portal" pay. Miners spent up to an hour and forty-eight minutes travelling to and from work along dark mine tunnels. It was, often, the most hazardous part of their day. The rate of accidents was high; the temperature change was extreme, exposing the miners to ailments not suffered by other workers. It was, at once, both a reasonable demand and one sure to unite the miners. Strikes rippled through the coal fields in March and April, 1943. On May 1, the President seized all the nation's coal mines, appointing crusty Harold Ickes, Secretary of the Interior, as coal administrator.

The miners stayed out of the mines sporadically in April,

concertedly for a time in June, and again sporadically in late October. Each time, their actions rivaled the battlefields for public attention. Each time, their actions backed up Lewis in the course of his negotiations with the government.

Editorials crackled with demands for the jailing of Lewis and for drafting strikers into the army. "Court martial is too good for Lewis while our boys die overseas," more than one editorial declaimed. Soldiers on far-flung shores were interviewed for their reactions to the coal strikes. Since they were far from well-informed as well as far from home, with few exceptions they condemned the strike and the strikers.

President Roosevelt threatened to draft the striking miners. But mineworkers shrugged this off with the observation, "You can't dig coal with bayonets." Union leaders, however, were caught in the unhappy predicament of favoring the demands of the miners while fearing the course taken by Lewis. Their fears were confirmed in mid-summer when an irate Congress passed over the President's veto the Smith-Connally Act. This Act empowered the President to seize struck facilities; punished by fine or imprisonment a strike at a plant in the Government's possession; required a 30-day cooling-off period following a strike notice; and prescribed that a strike vote be taken on the thirtieth day by the NLRB. Lewis was widely attacked in the labor movement for bringing on the passage of a "vicious anti-labor bill."

In October, the President once again seized the mines. This time, however, he authorized Secretary Ickes to negotiate directly with the mine union. On November 3, 1943, Lewis ordered the miners back to work, having negotiated a complicated settlement with Ickes. The $1.50-a-day increase secured by the miners fell within the Little Steel formula only because it was partially offset by an increase in the hours of work, achieved through a reduction of the lunch period, and because part of it was assigned to portal-to-portal pay.

The coal strike was followed by trouble on the railroads. A pay raise of eight cents an hour was awarded by a board convened under the Railway Labor Act. But this was vetoed by Economic Stabilization director Fred Vinson. He held that the award exceeded the Little Steel Formula. A strike vote was taken, with 98 percent voting in favor. December 30 was set as a strike deadline. Again headlines and editorials thundered condemnation. President Roosevelt ordered the Army to seize the railroads. It was, incidently, a popular move among railroad workers, some of whom favorably re-called the government's operation of the railroads during World War I. Also, it must be noted, that the employers—both in the mine and rail negotiations—had refused to budge, relying on the Little Steel formula to hold the line for them against proposed wage increases. The government, as the railroad workers and the miners expected, came up with a solution in the end. In January, 1944, a settlement was worked out that gave the railroad workers hourly increases ranging from four to ten cents an hour, plus an additional one to five cents an hour in place of overtime after forty hours of work in a week.

Other unions began pressing for wage increases. "Workers, war-weary and fearful about their post-war future seem to be grabbing any excuse for a strike these days," the *Wall Street Journal* informed its readers one summer day in 1944. As the war in Europe drew to a close, the unions urged the President to re-establish free collective bargaining within 60 days of the war's end. In February, 1945, the United Textile Workers became the first union to end its wartime no-strike policy officially. On August 19, 1945, four days after the surrender of Japan, President Harry S. Truman authorized voluntary wage increases that did not affect prices to become effective without WLB approval.

American trade unions came out of the war greatly strengthened. Union membership rose from about 10.5-million at Pearl Harbor to about 14.7 million when the war ended. The new industrial unions of the CIO were firmly entrenched in auto, rubber, steel and other mass production industries. The AF of L was stronger than ever before in the crafts and building and construction trades, and possessed strength in a large number of industrial plants. Union officials, as members of wartime advisory agencies, gained a prestige not previously enjoyed by the leaders of labor.

The unions also gained strength in the eyes of their members by winning their cases for wage gains before the War Labor Board. The Board corrected wage inequities, set equal pay for equal work for women workers, allowed a pattern of fringe benefits to emerge that had a tremendous influence on post World War II bargaining, and made increases to prevent substandard living. These gains were reflected in the increase in real earnings. Average real weekly earnings in manufacturing, $24 in terms of the 1935-39 price levels in 1939, rose to $28.12 in 1941 and reached a wartime peak of $36.72 in 1944. Real hourly earnings rose from 64 cents in 1939 to 69 cents in 1941 and peaked at 81 cents in 1944. The foundation for collective bargaining was set.

IX. Strike!

"THEY'VE CLOSED UP WILLOW RUN," declared the CIO *Economic Outlook* in the spring of 1945. "They gave the workers Army-Navy E's [military awards to civilians for excellence in production] and told them to go home because the Government and Mr. Ford didn't want the plant anymore. Nobody wants Willow Run, the $95 million factory that produced almost 9,000 Liberator bombers. Nobody wants the 51,950 pieces of machinery. . . . And nobody wants the more than 20,000 human beings who go with the plant."

Union members were worried about unemployment and a rising cost of living. Economists predicted five-to-eight-million unemployed within a year of the war's end. Older members uneasily recalled the union-busting campaigns that followed the end of World War I. These fears were reinforced by the flood of anti-union, restrictive labor legislation introduced in Congress. None was passed, but similar measures were enacted by a number of state legislatures, especially in states where industrialism was limited and unionism weak.

President Harry S. Truman pleaded for a continuance of the no-strike pledge, until his labor-management conference could solve some of the problems of a transition from the war economy to the new economy ahead. But the President's hopes for his labor-management conference were soon shattered. As soon as the war was over, labor chucked the non-strike pledge. During the last four-and-a-half months of 1945, man-days lost due to strikes shot up to 28,400,000, more than double the wartime peak of 1943, the year of the coal strikes.

In 1946, over four-and-a-half million workers marched on picket lines, a half-million more than the previous peak, in fateful 1919. One hundred thirteen million man-days of labor were lost, three times as many as in 1945 and the largest number ever. Strikes halted production in coal, auto, electric, steel, and other industries; maritime and rail transportation came to a halt.

Yet, for all the angry exchanges before newspaper reporters and the irate pounding on collective bargaining tables, strikers on the picket line frequently assumed a holiday air. Most workers simply "went fishing," taking time off to catch up on chores around the house or simply to relax. Unlike 1919, there was no stoking of revolutionary fires. *Fortune Magazine,* in November, aptly described the temper of the times: "The strikes and strike threats of 1945-46 generated violent emotions, but it was an impressive fact that for the first time a great wave of strikes stirred up almost no physical violence. The strikers of 1945-46 were not desperate men. On the public platform their leaders sounded off with booming phrases directed at the enemy Capital; but privately they, like the strikers, were calm, cool, even friendly warriors."

That the strikers were not desperate men, was due to the great changes in the economy brought about by the New Deal. The impact of unemployment, which rose over a million in 1945 and jumped to 2.3 million in 1946, was cushioned by unemployment insurance, which had not existed after World War I. The unemployed felt no great need to smash their way through picket lines to get jobs. Ex-soldiers built up little bitterness for an ungrateful country that might have caused labor-management clashes. The "52-20 Club" proved veterans with a full year of unemployment benefits at $20 a week. Others went to college on the GI Bill instead of entering a weakened labor market.

Management, too, contributed to the peacefulness of the 1946 strike wave by not contesting the right of the unions to exist. Few, if any firms, tried to open plant gates and operate in the face of a strike by their employees. Management's decision not to try to roll-back the unions to their uncertain, pre-war status was, in part, the unintentional result of government planning through taxation. Corporations that lost money during reconversion from production of war materials to normal production of peace-time goods could get returns on excess-profits taxes paid during the war. As *Fortune* pointed out: "A variety of factors makes strikes fairly cheap, in the short-range view, for some corporations. The excess-profits tax was in force until December 31, 1945; in the first eight months of the year the big war contractors had already made about as much money as they could hope to clear for the whole year; in some cases it was actually more profitable in terms of the 1945 balance sheet to shut down toward the end of the year rather than pay higher wages in advance of price relief."

The emergence of the CIO and the experience of the war years created a new kind of social consciousness among unionists, closely linked to collective bargaining. Though both the AF of L and the CIO were politically active, the new welfare unionism turned from government as the possible provider of social reform to collective bargaining for an expanding program of fringe benefits.

Welfare bargaining was shaped by a series of "pattern" settlements that washed over the economy in successive two- and three-year waves. These patterns were set in coal, steel, and auto as two new leaders of labor came to share the spotlight with John L. Lewis.

Philip Murray was born in Lanarkshire, Scotland, the son

of an Irish immigrant coal miner. His father, William Murray, was active in the Scottish trade union movement. On Christmas Day, 1902, the 16-year-old Philip and his father arrived in the United States as an advance party for the rest of the Murray clan. They wound up in Westmoreland County, Pennsylvania, where the young Murray shoveled enough coal to fill three mine cars a day at a dollar a car.

The young Murray first came to the attention of his fellow workers when he smacked a "weigh boss" suspected of cheating at the tipple, the point where coal brought out of the mines was tipped onto storage piles or into waiting rail cars. Each carload coming out of the mine was credited to a miner's team. Since pay was calculated on the basis of tonnage mined, cheating by the weigh boss was serious business. One of the union's earliest demands was for the right to have a miner check out the weigh boss.

Later, the miners struck and put the lanky 18-year-old Philip Murray at the head of a deputation to talk with the manager of the mine. The next day the Murrays were dispossessed from a company-owned house. They went to live in a tent, hastily erected by the striking miners. When hunger ended the strike, Philip Murray was personally escorted to the County line and told never to return.

The Murrays, like other miners barred from this or that mine because of union activity, moved on. They relocated in Allegheny County, where Philip again found work in a mine. This time it was a union-organized mine. He became active in the UMW and rose rapidly in District Five of the UMW, which covers Allegheny County and the rich Pittsburgh coal seam. By 1912, at 26, he was an international Board member and four years later, president of the District. Lewis made Murray a vice-president of the UMW in 1920.

Lewis also assigned Murray to the Steel Workers Organizing Committee. As a lad, Murray played an indifferent game of soccer but his team mates quickly learned that he was an excellent manager. The same talent soon made Murray the

George Harrison (left), leader of the AF of L Peace Delegation shakes hands with CIO leader, David Dubinsky while Philip Murray (center) and James Carey (second from right) look on at a conference to bring peace between the two warring labor organizations.

undisputed head of the steel union and—after Lewis's resignation—of the CIO. He was a gentle man, but firm.

Murray's temperament was admirably suited to the wartime transition of the CIO from the blustery, near-revolutionary union of the sit-down era to the corporate welfarist CIO of the postwar era. As John Chamberlain noted in *Life* in 1946, "The Murray mind is not a speculative mind and the Murray psychology is not made for revolution." Murray was a moderate.

The CIO president was influenced by the labor-management-public cooperativism of the Papal encyclicals *Rerum Novarum* (1891) and *Quadragesimo Anno* (1931). These two statements of Catholic philosophy spell out the Church's basic approach to social and economic questions. He was interested in the post-World War II German experiments in

131

co-determination, in which German trade unionists served as company directors along with representatives of management. Industrial democracy, Murray argued in a book co-authored by Morris Cooke, *Organized Labor and Production,* depended on collective bargaining with labor organizations, on one side, "able to regard the interests of the industry as a whole"; and, on the other side, organizations of employers "prepared to assume the responsibilities of economic statesmanship."

"As younger and better-trained men rise into positions of industrial leadership," wrote Murray and Cooke, "there is multiplying evidence of the infiltration of social-mindedness into the stubborn tissue of business self-interest. We see great labor unions taking seriously the idea of responsibility for continued production."

Murray's outlook also encompassed the welfarism of the needle trades unions with their emphasis on employer-financed, union-controlled health and welfare programs. As McAllister Coleman pointed out, Murray "was talking more in the quiet voice of Sidney Hillman than in the sonorous tones of Lewis."

Murray's, however, was a narrow vision, more akin to the craft unionists than to the visionaries of the Knights of Labor, the Wobblies, and early CIO rebels. His outlook encompassed an industry, or the economy, as seen industry by industry. It dovetailed neatly with postwar developments in collective bargaining.

Walter P. Reuther is of the new breed of trade unionists, visionaries who see trade unionists, not employers, as taking on the role of economic and social statesmanship. He is to this day the leading voice of the new social unionism.

Walter P. Reuther was born on Labor Day, 1907, in Wheeling, West Virginia. His grandfather fled Germany for the freedom of the United States. His father, Valentine Reuther, inherited a binding sense of moral duty, which he passed on to his sons along with a lesser measure of his de-

132

votion to the socialism of Eugene Victor Debs.

Valentine Reuther was a brewery worker and ardent trade unionist. On Sunday afternoon, he set up informal debates among his boys. Ted was the oldest and the only one who did not go into the labor movement. Victor, Roy, and Walter were all destined to be active in the UAW. The Reuthers argued the social questions of the day—pacifism, socialism, capital punishment, women in industry, and so on. Their father also passed on his conviction that every man ought to have a trade.

So, Walter quit high school in his third year to take a job as an apprentice toolmaker. He soon rebelled at having to work Sundays, organized a protest and was fired for his pains. He went to Detroit where he broke in as a tool and die maker at Briggs, an auto parts manufacturer. He worked the night shift for 85 cents an hour. He then went on to Ford where he received $1.10 an hour as a full-fledged tool and die worker.

In 1932, the fiery redhead campaigned for Norman Thomas, the Socialist Party candidate for the Presidency. A year later, he was fired by Ford for union activity. Then, Walter and Victor decided to take a tour around the world, using their small store of savings as a start. It was the grand tour—but where young college students on their year

Representatives of the UAW, at the left side, meet at the bargaining table with representatives of the Ford Motor Company for contract negotiations.

abroad visited museums or bicycled through the English countryside, the Reuthers toured England's auto plants, textile mills, and coal pits. They arrived in Berlin the day before the Reichstag fire. That German parliamentary building was destroyed by fire on February 27, 1933. Later, it was believed to have been set by the Nazis, who had just come into power but who had not yet consolidated their political position. At the time, however, a Dutch Communist, Marinus van der Lubbe, was charged with the crime, tried and beheaded. It was the occasion for a show trial providing considerable public hysteria, which helped Hitler establish his dictatorship firmly. The Reuther brothers lived with anti-Nazi students and helped a few escape over the border into Switzerland.

The brothers then went on to work 16 months in an auto plant in Gorki, Russia, a city built for the Soviet government by the Ford Motor Company. At the time, there was generally an uncritical attitude towards Russia and Stalin's totalitarian rule, which opinion the Reuthers shared. By the time they left Gorki, the Reuthers were disenchanted with Stalin and have been outspoken opponents of totalitarianism ever since.

On the way back, they stopped off for short visits in India, where they caught a glimpse of Mahatma Gandhi's movement for Indian independence, and in Japan, where they saw something of Japanese militarism. As Irving Howe and B. J. Widick note in their book, *The UAW and Walter Reuther,* "No one could have asked for a more direct education in modern realities."

Back in Detroit, the Reuthers played a leading role in the sit-downs. Walter as a volunteer organizer, began amalgamating the tiny and scattered west side UAW locals into one big local union. During 1937, the Local grew from 8,000 to 30,000 members. The Reuther brothers were also in action at Flint, helping to guide the sit-downers to their victory over General Motors. Walter was one of the men severely beaten at the Ford overpass in 1941. He first attracted national attention just before World War II by his suggestion that the idle facilities of the auto companies might be used to manufacture fighter planes. During the war, Walter Reuther became head of the UAW's General Motors Department.

When the UAW opened its first post-war negotiations with the auto companies, Reuther convinced the union executive board that the union ought to take the companies on "one at a time." (It's a strategy, incidentally, that still prevails.) General Motors was the company picked. Reuther's leadership of the GM strike, which started on November 21, 1945, and involved 200,000 workers in 96 plants across the country, catapulted him into the presidency of the union a few months later.

George Romney, now Governor of Michigan and former head of American Motors, once said, "Walter Reuther is the most dangerous man in Detroit because no one is more skillful in bringing about revolution without seeming to disturb the existing forms of society."

Reuther's insistence on a wage increase without any increase in the price of cars made him labor's chief spokesman in the first round of collective bargaining that followed the end of World War II. Taking advantage of a recent Presidential order allowing voluntary wage increases where there were no compensatory price increases, Reuther insisted that General Motors open its books to prove or disprove the union's contention that the auto company could grant a 30 percent wage increase without any increase in auto prices.

It was a radical demand as Romney's description of Reuther's major skill would indicate. The Reuther-UAW demand injected organized labor directly into corporate decision-making, if not into the still broader area of economic planning. If the UAW's case could be upheld, the wage gain would be a gain in real wages. A halt to climbing prices would have given other workers a chance to catch up to the rising cost of living. To clinch the matter, the UAW offered to forego a wage increase if it could be shown from an examination of GM's books that a wage increase could not be granted.

Behind the UAW's fight with General Motors loomed whatever is—or was—left of the radical impulse to remake American society in labor's image. And it seemed for a moment that the country was on the brink of a new order of things. The President asserted at a press conference that the ability to pay was always relevant when wage increases were under consideration. GM went to the heart of the dispute when it challenged a Presidential Fact Finding Board's competence to pass on future profits and rejected the union's effort to make its price policy a collective bargaining issue. After GM stormed out of the fact-finding hearings, the Board recommended on January 10, 1946, an hourly increase of 19½ cents, asserting that it was well within the Corporation's ability to pay. GM rejected the recommendations.

The spirit of CIO Auto Workers' members is high as the 1946 strike enters its 100th day, making it the longest strike in automobile history.

WIDE WORLD PHOTOS

Collective bargaining in other industries, however, forced the government's hand. On January 15, 1946, 200,000 electrical workers struck, followed by an equal number of packinghouse workers on the next day. Five days later, 750,000 steelworkers shut down the steel industry. But Philip Murray made it clear that his concern was with wages, not prices.

Industry used the strikes as a way of pressuring Washington to relax the price line. When U.S. Steel was finally assured of a five dollar a ton price increase, Benjamin Fairless quickly settled with Murray. The steel strike ended after 30 days with the 18½ cent wage increase suggested by the President. The price increase, acording to the *Chicago-Sun*, netted the steel companies $435,000,000 additional income at a cost of only $185,000,00 in wage boosts.

The UAW, then, had no other choice but to give in on the open-books issue. After 113 days, the GM strike ended on March 13, 1946, with the 18½ cent wage boost set by steel. The other major strikes of that year were pretty much settled on the same pattern. Price controls were lifted on June 30. The postwar wage and price spiral was firmly set.

The cost of negotiated wage and benefit packages proved to be useful justifications for raising prices. As writer, Daniel Bell has shown, postwar strikes and resulting wage boosts became an excuse for raising prices and lowering the break-even point—the lowest level of production that will sustain no loss—for industry. Prices were then "administered" with this in mind. Public assent, or acceptance, however, was still essential before prices could be raised. The unions were often blamed for rising prices, a fact that contributed to management's easy acceptance of collective bargaining as a valuable aid to corporate pricing policies.

This development was not without its advantages for organized workers. Wage and benefit packages were heavy with gains undreamed of before World War II—including vacation and holiday pay, noncontributory pension plans, health and other welfare benefits, supplementary unemployment benefits (a significant step towards a guaranteed annual wage or salary), and early retirement benefits among others.

But labor paid a price. Weak unions, such as those in textiles, retail stores and quasi-public services (hospital workers, for example), were unable to match the gains won by labor's giants. These gains, in turn, were used by industry to justify price increases (over which workers had no say) that fell hardest upon the poor and ill-organized workers. In *The Other America,* Michael Harrington detailed the costs born by the non-working and working poor because of the imbalances created by a high-profit corporate society.

Viewed in this light, the 1945 GM strike was a major defeat for organized labor. The unions lost an opportunity for deepening worker-involvement in the decisions that affect their lives. Significantly, the UAW under Reuther's leadership has returned to the question of pricing in negotiations after negotiations, insisting that wage increases need not result in price boosts. So far, however, their persistence has not been notably successful, although by making the public aware of the issue the union may have acted as a damper on price rises. Still, the key question of worker involvement in corporate planning has yet to be answered.

X. Merger

John L. Lewis's last major strike was the coal walkout of 1946. That year, the mine operators were perfectly willing to accept the prevailing 18½-cent package. (Lewis was one of the few labor leaders to oppose the continuation of price control.) But a rumbling Lewis was not about to be so restrained. He demanded, in addition to the wage hike, a royalty on each ton of coal mined to finance health and welfare services in the mining camps.

The coal mines shut down on April 1, 1946, as a result of the mine owner's rejection of the union's demands. There was a two-week truce in May and the Federal Government seized the mines just before the truce expired. Lewis and Secretary of the Interior Julius A. Krug sat down to bargain on the terms of the government's operation of the mines.

The Federal mine administrator and Lewis soon reached an agreement that ultimately became the foundation for coal peace when the mines were back in private hands. It provided for the establishment of two benefit funds, a welfare and retirement fund jointly administered by coal management and the union, and a medical and hospital fund controlled by the union. The funds were financed by a five-cent

Non-union miners in Clearfield, Pennsylvania defied the strike called by John L. Lewis and went back to work. These strikebreakers, fearful of union strikers, carried guns on the job.

royalty on each ton of coal mined. A federal mine-safety code was to be adopted, the miners were to get an 18½-cent hourly wage increase as well as improved vacation benefits.

Late in the fall, Lewis again threatened to pull out the mineworkers, claiming a violation of his agreement with Krug. Federal Judge T. Alan Goldsborough issued a temporary restraining order forbidding the strike. But the mineworkers quit work anyway. Lewis and the union were found in contempt of court. The mine chief was fined $10,000 and the union $3,500,000, the largest financial penalty ever imposed on a union in the history of the United States. The union lost an appeal to the Supreme Court, which, however, reduced the penalty to $700,000 on condition that the union purge itself of contempt within a reasonable time. The union did so by calling off the strike.

When the mines were returned to the mine owners at the end of June, 1947, after the expiration of the Smith-Connally Act, Lewis secured a new agreement raising daily wages from $11.85 for nine hours to $13.05 for eight. The royalty benefit was raised from five cents to ten cents a ton.

Over the years, this has increased to 40 cents a ton.

By the end of fiscal 1966, the funds paid out almost $2 billion in benefits, roughly half in pensions and half in hospital and medical benefits. The working miner had come a long way since the day when his children had to scrabble for coal at the pithead.

The royalty on coal, strictly speaking, was not an innovation. During the 1930's, the needle-trades had established a similar welfare-benefit system, employer financed, union controlled. But their welfare funds were financed by a tax on payroll; the miners' by a tax on coal produced. This gave the union an interest in improving mechanization of the mines. As J. B. S. Hardman noted in summarizing Lewis's career in *Labor History* (Winter, 1961), "Thanks to Lewis, the traditionally 'sick' coal industry is doing well. For decades Lewis had urged the captains of the coal industry to behave like 'capitalists,' to consolidate, modernize, and mechanize. The leader of the coal miners taught free enterprise the art of enterprising." But though the health of the industry has been good, this has not been the case for all miners.

Mechanization has driven the small "truck" mine, along with a good many miners, out of business. "It is better," Lewis once declared, "to have a half million men working in the industry at good wages, high standards of living, than it is to have a million men working in the industry in poverty and degradation."

Today, 160,000 men mine coal, a number far short of Lewis's "half-million" optimum. The modernization of the mines enabled miners to work more efficiently and more safely. But it did so at the cost of high unemployment in the region of Appalachia. Mechanized mines need fewer mine workers and greater seams of coal. Small and marginal mines cannot compete with the larger and more efficient ones—at least not under present conditions that allow the mine companies to strip away the earth to get at the black gold beneath without, however, having to account for the damage done to the land and its streams. So, just as the giant diesel-powered shovels scar the countryside, the improvements in mine mechanization have disrupted the mining communities. In Appalachia, a small number of highly-paid workers and prosperous corporate giants exist alongside gaunt pockets of poverty.

King Coal exacted his tribute over the years, creating a people with little education, ignorant and innocent about the outside world. Mine towns never dared tax the absentee mine owners enough to provide a decent education, nor for the retraining necessary if unemployed workers were to get other jobs. (It took union power to get money from the owners to cover much needed medical facilities for the miners and their families.) Many an ex-miner left Appalachia to seek work elsewhere only to return having discovered that his proud skills wouldn't do in the steel mills or auto plants. Since Appalachia was for so many years a one-industry region, a miner's sons could not turn to Uncle Frank at the machine shop, or young Uncle George at the electronics factory for a job, or an introduction to a job. There were only the mines.

Coal miner indicates his opinion of the court ruling against John L. Lewis and the United Mine Workers' Union. The union was fined $1,400,000 and Lewis fined $20,000 for criminal contempt of court.

UNITED PRESS INTERNATIONAL

Lewis's return to the coal miners was a kind of turning inwards and was aptly symbolic for the decade that followed World War II. First, the CIO turned inward to confront the problem of Communist control over certain key unions; second, the AF of L turned inward to cleanse itself of racketeering. Both developments were spurred by pressures from outside the labor movement.

While the major employers did not challenge labor's right to exist, small manufacturers and little businessmen were fearful of what they considered the "monopoly power of the unions." This fear was reflected in the so-called "right-to-work" laws passed in some 21 states, mostly Southern and mostly where unions were noticeably weak, and in the passage of the 1946 Taft-Hartley Act. The common feature of this legislation is the restriction placed on the unions. The union shop and maintenance-of-membership clauses in union contracts, as well as the closed shop, which is forbidden in Taft-Hartley, are outlawed.

The new laws also provided that it is not an unfair labor practice for an employer to express his views on any subject unless it contains a threat of reprisal or promise of benefit. This "free speech" provision, in practice, allowed employers in non-union industries a wide latitude. It did not mean much in an industrial state, such as New York, but in the South generally it has meant the death of many an organizing campaign.

The Textile Workers Union's experience in the South offers a good example of what this sort of anti-union pressure did to unionization. In 1952, the Textile Union filed unfair-labor charges against Anchor Rome Mills in Rome, Georgia. Seven months later, the general counsel for the NLRB issued a complaint. Eight months later, the trial examiner issued his intermediate report finding illegal coercion on the part of the employer. After another eight months —almost two years later—the NLRB upheld the trial examiner's findings. Meanwhile, the union had disintegrated in the face of the employer's constant though illegal pressure on his workers.

The tactics an employer can bring to bear on union activists are varied. They may be fired outright but more often they are laid off in slack-time first, in complete disregard for their seniority. It is customary—reinforced by union contracts—to lay off workers in accordance with their time on the job. Short-time workers go first. Union members may find themselves transferred willy-nilly from job to job within the plant. This form of harassment is much resented since the move is often a demotion or a shift from a good job to a bad or dirty job. Also, workers active in the union may lose out on overtime, choice of vacation-time, or any other of the privileges at management's disposal. Time and time again, as a result of such practices, labor's drives to organize in the South faltered and failed.

Meanwhile, within the CIO a fierce fight raged over the expulsion of Communists. They were finally expelled for going against the political decision of the CIO to endorse Harry S. Truman for his second term in the 1948 election. The Communists had backed Henry A. Wallace's third party effort.

The AF of L, in 1953, began cleaning its house of corruption. A three-year fight along the nation's east coast ended with the clean-up of crime on the waterfront. Later exposures of union racketeering by the Senate Select Committee on Improper Activities in the Labor and Management Field, chaired by Senator John L. McClellan, led to further expulsions.

The election of Dwight David Eisenhower as President in 1952 changed the climate for labor in Washington. President Eisenhower's appointments, for instance, to the National Labor Relations Board changed the majority from one friendly to labor to one friendly to business. Moreover, the Republican presence in the White House meant that Administration pressures in major collective bargaining disputes would change. During Eisenhower's years, settlement of labor disputes tended to be pro-business, though not in the old sense anti-labor. This political change forced the AF of L and the CIO into greater cooperation with government and business.

AF of L and CIO rivalry had reached a dead end during this time. For example, where competition once increased union membership and worker benefits—groups of workers often called in both AF of L and CIO organizers, set them bidding against one another, then chose the union that delivered. This was no longer the case. "No union" voters were winning in representation elections where a united organizing drive might have scored a union victory. So, if AF of L and the CIO worked out a no-raiding pact. It was, as it turned out, a step towards merger.

The Communists, once a major AF of L objection to unity, were out of the CIO; the racketeers, a major CIO objection to unity, were out, or on the way out of the AF of L. Lewis's old protégés, Green and Murray, died in 1952. George Meany succeeded Green and Walter Reuther succeeded Murray. Each at the time wanted a united labor movement. On

John L. Lewis and Hugh White, President of Illinois' UMW after inspection of Orient #2 mine disaster in which 119 men lost their lives.

December 5, 1955, the AF of L and the CIO became one, bringing together in one House of Labor some 16 million workers, over 85 percent of all union members.

The merger of the two powerful wings of American labor, however, would have been much more difficult than it was without the presence of a Bronx plumber, George Meany. A burly, ham-fisted, massive figure, with a slight limp from an old heel injury, Meany seemed to be the least likely union leader to upset the ancient traditions of the craft-oriented Federation. He was born into a union family in 1894 on the Upper West Side of Manhattan. His father headed a large plumber's local and "Mike Meany's boy," after a year in high school quit to become an apprentice. A journeyman plumber at 22, Meany helped to support his recently widowed mother and seven brothers and sisters. He became a plumbers' business agent at 28 and thereafter his rise within the AF of L hierarchy was as steady and sure as the skills of his old trade.

By the 1930's, George Meany was the president of the New York State Federation of Labor. He was also a crony of Joe "The Waxer" Ryan, boss of the International Longshoremen's Association and of the New York City Central Trades Council. But Meany quickly showed his independence, when he tangled with the Longshoremen's leader over the candidacy of Fiorello LaGuardia for Mayor of New York City, whom Meany supported against Ryan's wishes.

Nonetheless, Meany was considered a "safe" candidate for the AF of L secretary-treasurership in 1939, and it was no suprise when he became head of the Federation in 1952. A blunt man, Meany wastes little time with subtleties. Once faced with the necessity to act against corruption, he moved without hesitation. He bounced his old friend Joe Ryan and the then-corrupt ILA out of the House of Labor. Once the union had been purged of its corrupt elements, Meany brought them back to the Federation.

As a craftsman, Meany enjoyed the confidence of the building and construction trades unions. They were, by and

146

"All Trades—All Crafts—All Colors—All Creeds—Together!"—this was the slogan on December 5, 1955 as George Meany's AF of L and Walter Reuther's CIO became one united "House of Labor."

147

large, reluctant to have the Federation merge with the CIO. The craft unionists believe in autonomy—that is, esentially, each union should mind its own business. The old AF of L Constitution granted few powers of chastisement, discipline or enforcement of policy to its top officers. Meany, however, believed in a strong Federation, with powers to set erring affiliates right. His willingness to accept constitutional provisions put forth by the CIO in pre-merger talks, strengthening the powers of the executive council of the merged group, won him the support of the CIO unions. Meany persuaded the craft-unions to go along; after all, he was to be president and didn't they have confidence in him?

Merger capped the coming of age of organized labor. Today, the unions are powerful social institutions within their own right. Still, organized labor has not solved all of the problems working men and women face in an increasingly complex world. The old debate—and in many ways a fruitful one—continues between those unionists who believe that trade unions ought to concentrate on representing their members as best they can and those who believe that the trade union movement has both broader responsibilities and a social vision essential to the creation of a better society. Only the future can tell how that debate will be resolved— if ever.

A Supplementary Reading List

For the reader who would like to explore the history of American labor further, I would recommend the following books as a beginning:

BROOKS, THOMAS R., *Toil and Trouble: A History of American Labor,* New York, Delacorte Press, 1964.

CHRISTIE, ROBERT A., *Empire in Wood,* Ithaca, New York, Cornell University Press, 1956.

COLEMAN, MCALISTER, *Men and Coal,* New York, Farrar & Rinehart, 1943.

HOWE, IRVING, and WIDICK, B. J., *The UAW and Walter Reuther,* New York, Random House, 1949.

TYLER, GUS, *The Labor Revolution,* New York, The Viking Press, 1967.

Index

150

A Note About the Author

A graduate *cum laude* from Harvard University, THOMAS R. BROOKS has been a labor editor for several publications, including *Business Week Magazine*. His articles have appeared in *The New York Times Magazine, The Reporter, Commentary, Reader's Digest* and many others. His previous book, TOIL AND TROUBLE: *A History of American Labor,* was listed as one of the 100 Best Books of 1965 by *The New York Times.*